The *Sensus Fidelium*

The *Sensus Fidelium*

With Special Reference to the Thought of Blessed John Henry Newman

Kathleen Kirk

GRACEWING

First published in 2010

Gracewing
2 Southern Avenue
Leominster
Herefordshire HR6 0QF

ISBN 978 0 85244 746 8

Typeset by Action Publishing Technology Ltd
Gloucester GL1 5SR

Contents

Acknowledgements

Material from the following works is reproduced by kind permission of Continuum International Publishing Group:
  On Consulting the Faithful in Matters of Doctrine, ed. John Coulson (London: Geoffrey Chapman, 1961);
  Catechism of the Catholic Church (London: Geoffrey Chapman, 1994);
  Yves Congar, *Lay People in the Church* (London: Geoffrey Chapman, 1957).

Material from John Paul II, *The Theology of the Body* (Boston, MA: Pauline Books & Media, 1997), reproduced by kind permission of Libreria Editrice Vaticana.

If, through inadvertence, any rights still surviving have not been acknowledged, pardon is sought and apology made. A correction will be made in any reprint of this book.

In addition, I wish to acknowledge my indebtedness and express my gratitude to the following:

Michael Blades, formerly Principal of Plater College, at whose instigation I undertook the thesis on which this book is based. This was at the completion of my course as a theology student at the college.

Gregory Glazov, then Theology Tutor at Plater, who supervized my work.

Lincoln's Inn and the Newman Trust who helped with my finances.

Fr William Wright, OSB of Ampleforth, for his interest, guidance and encouragement, especially relating to my studies of Pope John Paul II's *Theology of the Body*.

Not least to my friend, Liz Higgins, who dealt with the technology of pre-publication e-mail correspondence for me and did so with unfailing promptness and good humour.

A Necessary Introduction

The Author's Aims

I need to alert my readers to a difference in character which they will encounter between the earlier chapters of my book and Chapter Seven. As the reader will see, the earlier chapters are concerned, broadly speaking, with the nature of the *sensus fidelium*, its subjects, its history, the views of some post-Vatican II theologians on the matter, Newman's thought as applied to those views and *On Consulting the Faithful in Matters of Doctrine*, being his own essay on the *sensus fidelium*. Most of the theologians, examples of whose opinions I give, write in the aftermath of Pope Paul VI's 1968 encyclical 'On the Regulation of Birth' *(Humanae Vitae)*. Many of them attempt, by a manipulation, so it seems to me, of the doctrine of the *sensus fidelium*, to give a theological justification for the encyclical's rejection among the laity. What I most wish to make clear in this introduction is this: All the exposition briefly described above and contained in the earlier chapters showing, with the help of Newman and other authorities, what the *sensus fidelium* is and what it is not, are written in the service of Chapter Seven, and my hope is that they will be read in that way. In that chapter I discuss the question of the *sensus fidelium* in relation to opposition to the magisterium, with

Humanae Vitae at the centre of my argument. At that stage my observations become a study of the *sensus fidelium* in relation to marriage and sexuality based upon the teaching contained in Pope John Paul II's 'Theology of the Body'. Crucial to that teaching is the existence of marriage as one of the sacraments of the Church (and outside the Church as having a sacramental character). I contend that it is from awareness of this sacramentality that a study of the rightfulness or otherwise of contraception should begin. I try to show how there does not at present exist among the faithful as a whole a *sensus fidelium* of a truly Christian depth as far as marriage and sexuality are concerned; that is to say, I find lacking in this area the qualities of a genuine *sensus fidelium* as they have been identified in my earlier chapters. This surely means that further formation of this Christian sense among us is necessary. It is for the purposes of that formation that I commend the theology of Pope John Paul mentioned above.

I have another, and underlying, purpose which is to uphold the teaching of the Church on marriage and sexuality, a teaching that I fear has come under suspicion and into disrepute of late. There seems to be a notion abroad, both inside and outside the Church, that she has got it a little wrong somehow, or even entirely wrong. As I remarked, we begin in this matter with the recollection of marriage as a sacrament; we then ask, 'Does the conjugal act partake of this sacramental character and, if so, in what precise way?' The answer I arrive at is deduced from what Pope John Paul says about the liturgical aspect of marriage and from a concept which he names as 'the language of the body'. Putting it very briefly here, I understand him to say that, following upon the ritual of the exchange of marriage vows, there is in the domestic marital act an uninterrupted continuation of liturgical language by means of the language of the body. The deduction I make is that the marital act belongs not simply to the sacrament but specifically to the sacramental rite; or rather, that act is the form which the rite finally takes throughout married life. If that is so then it seems to me that the integral conjugal act must needs be the sole valid expression (in the physical sense) of our sexuality. I explain in my text why I say this of the 'integral conjugal act' since I argue that contraception would prejudice ritual effectiveness. Human sexuality having been claimed for the ritual purposes of the sacrament how can any lesser use to which it may be put, whether within marriage or otherwise, retain any meaning? The unique validity of the conjugal act is, of course, what the Church has always taught, howbeit that the theology of Pope John Paul is not yet general apostolic teaching. When that does come about (and there are signs that it is on the way) then we shall begin to see that the Church, because her teaching on the rights and wrongs of sexual behaviour all stems from the fact of Our Lord's establishment of marriage as a sacrament, far from having got it wrong, has got it supremely right.

Chapter One

Who are 'The Faithful?' Why Do They Need a Sense of the Faith?

When we speak of the *sensus fidelium,* the 'sense of the faithful', that instinct for supernatural truth and unerring testimony to Christian doctrine, who are 'the faithful' we have in mind? Some commentators lend support to the pleasing image of 'the faithful' as the simple, theologically unlettered laity whose witness to the truth at a time of crisis puts the intellegentia and the episcopate to shame. Yves Congar, in his *Lay People in the Church,* asserts:

> It is unquestionable that throughout the first half of the fourth century the faithful people resisted Arianism and its by-products, a heresy of intellectuals that was often accepted by the bishops themselves, whether as theologians or because they followed imperial inclinations.[1]

Congar names Newman's *On Consulting the Faithful in Matters of Doctrine* and J. Lebreton's 'Le désaccord de la foi populaire et de la théologie savante . . .'[2] as examples of how certain Catholic historians have written of the faithful witness of the people during that epoch; in the case of Newman's work, such witness being in spite of the infidelity of the bishops and, in Lebreton's, against the rash speculations of the *savants*. Furthermore, the belief expressed by Karl Rahner that the faith of the *Volk* is closer to the original experience of revelation than reflexive forms such as theology[3] seems to support our image of the superior witness of the layman. So most of all does Newman when we hear him affirm: 'The humblest and meanest among Christians may defend the faith against the whole Church, if need arise ... and has nothing to limit him in his protest except his intellectual capacity for making it.'[4] Who but a member of the laity, we think, can this 'humblest and meanest' of Christians be?

But it would be too romantic a view that saw the *sensus fidelium* as being most typically at work in the gallant testimony of the embattled layman. It will be seen as our study proceeds that the theology of the *sensus fidelium,* as seen in scriptural sources, the Church Fathers and the successive Councils of the Church shows the *sensus fidelium* as a gift which the general faithful share with the holders of office. Even so, a preoccupation with the *sensus fidelium* as a charism of the laity will be observed in the writings of our contemporary theologians, even while showing themselves aware that it belongs to the Church as a whole. But, before we come to these, let us consider why we Christians should need an inner 'sense' of the faith when we would expect that history could give us access, in an objective manner, to the knowledge which we need of the deposit of faith. We do this with the help of Newman's analysis of the Vincentian principle.

Newman on the Vincentian Principle

What does this gift, the *sensus fidelium* consist of? It can be described (though fuller definitions will be given later) as an instinct for the inner coherence of the various propositions of the faith; a spontaneous inward inclination on the part of the Mystical Body. So it is a supernatural gift of discernment. But cannot the truths of the faith be ascertained at any given time in accordance with the well-known adage of St Vincent of Lérins: *Quod semper, quod ubique, quod ab omnibus*, that is to say: Christianity is what has been held 'always, everywhere and by all'? The answer has to do with the phenomenon of the development of doctrine, and with certain limits and defects of the Vincentian principle. In pointing out these defects Newman says that, although the adage 'Christianity is what has been held always, everywhere, and by all' offers 'an intelligible principle and wears a reasonable air', it is difficult to apply in particular cases. He considers the rule more serviceable in determining what is not, rather than what is, Christianity. He decries its use to exclude any doctrine not referable to the earliest times. 'The Rule of Vincent is not of a mathematical or demonstrative character, but moral, and requires practical judgement and good sense to apply it.' Newman was always against a too facile solution of perplexities, a feeling to which his *Essay on the Development of Christian Doctrine* bears testimony (the perplexity in this case being how to reconcile the fact of a once for all revelation by Jesus Christ to the first Apostles with the subsequent appearance of doctrines which on the face of things were not easily ascribable to the primitive revelation); the *quod semper* dictum had lent itself to such facile solutions. The solution is achieved 'by cutting off and casting away as corruptions all usages, ways, opinions and tenets, which have not the sanction of primitive times.' Newman's arguments have in mind the difficulties of Anglicans in accepting certain Catholic doctrines which they regard as unwarrantable and latter day additions, an attitude not unknown among Catholics themselves. As Newman remarks: 'It [the Vincentian argument] affords a ready loophole for such as do not wish to be persuaded, of which both Protestants and Romanists are not slow to avail themselves'. Newman concludes his argument on the Vincentian dictum as follows:

> It does not seem possible, then, to avoid the conclusion that ... true as the dictum of Vincentius must be considered in the abstract, and possible as its application might be in his own age [itself 'Early Church'] ... it is hardly available now, or effective of any satisfactory result. The solution it offers is as difficult as the original problem.[5]

It is obvious that the Vincentian principle has to do with the objective content of the dogmas of the Church, whereas, as many theologians emphasize, the *sensus fidelium* is intrinsic to faith and has a subjective constituent.

The Rule of Faith

Similarly, it might be asked, But what of the Rule of Faith? Does not this, as does the *sensus fidelium*, tell us what we should believe? How do the two differ from or relate to each other?

If the Rule of Faith is the explicit formulation, in one way or another, of the content of what is taught, believed and professed by the Church of Jesus Christ, and the *sensus fidelium* a kind of instinct, as Newman tells us, in the Mystical Body, one might say that the difference, and the relationship, is that one is objective, the other subjective. In his work on the *sensus fidelium* Newman, in order to explain that instinct, quotes from Möhler's *Symbolique:* '*Ce sentiment commun, cette conscience de L'Eglise est la tradition dans le sens subjective du mot.*' ('This common feeling, this conscience of the Church, is tradition in the subjective sense of the word.') Möhler goes on to explain the nature of tradition considered from the subjective point of view as the Christian sense existing in and transmitted by the Church; this sense is such that it can never be separated from the truths it contains, being formed from and by those truths.[6]

It can be seen that explicit faith statements are insufficient. They cannot embrace all the fullness, depth and nuances of the faith and its practice. They are intended to be brief summaries and to serve a practical purpose. Communion in the Christian faith needs a normative, common language of faith uniting all in the same confession. From the earliest times, the Church also wished 'to gather the essential elements of her faith into organic and articulated summaries intended especially for candidates for baptism.'[7]

We shall see how Yves Congar says of the *sensus fidelium* that 'there is a gift of God (of the Holy Spirit) which relates to the twofold reality, objective and subjective, of faith'.[8] That is, it both pertains to the content of faith and is that charism by means of which we believe. There is nothing in the Rule of Faith, standing by itself, which would cause or enable us to believe what it contains.

Chapter Two

Post-Vatican II Reflections on the *Sensus Fidelium*

Newman and Vatican II

Why should the thought of the Second Vatican Council also bring Blessed John Henry Newman to mind? The Council opened in 1962, seventy-two years after Newman's death. Yet he had entertained hopes and wishes for the Church which in our time have been fulfilled in the measures and recommendations of Vatican II, most importantly in its Dogmatic Constitution on the Church, *Lumen Gentium*. The Council placed emphasis on certain doctrines and ecclesial realities which did not, in the years following the Council of Trent, appear much to the fore in the Church at large, though perceived and cultivated by Newman himself.[1] In particular, he was convinced that the dogma of papal infallibility, as propounded by the First Vatican Council, would be completed and placed in a wider ecclesial context by a future Council, as indeed has happened with *Lumen Gentium*. What is more, Newman's theology as an Anglican was based on a profound study of Scripture and the Fathers of the Church. Ian Ker makes this comment:

> Since the teaching of the Second Vatican Council, which arose out of and which in turn stimulated a return to the

sources of the Church's theology, Newman's deeply scriptural and patristic thought has come into its own among Catholic theologians.[2]

There has been another important change which would have been welcomed by Newman. He and his contemporaries were under the constant and inhibiting surveillance of Rome in all they wrote, while we in our time enjoy much more freedom in this respect; a general libertarian culture has now developed in the Church as being thought to accord with 'the spirit of the Council'. The present-day theologians whose reflections on the *sensus fidelium* I am about to consider, have different aims from those of Newman in his treatment of the subject, giving it a different slant and a wider scope. They are often concerned to urge the putting into effect of conciliar measures where they feel this practical implementation is lacking.

To say that our contemporaries' treatment has a wider scope is not to say that Newman's thought is in any way impoverished. As was remarked above, many of the theological themes in which these authors set their reflections, themes introduced or stressed by the Council, are to be found in Newman's writings. Along with this it always has to be remembered, with regard to Newman's works, that most were occasional, and all sprang from the circumstances and preoccupations of his own life, *On Consulting the Faithful in Matters of Doctrine* (which contains his teaching on the *sensus fidelium*) most poignantly so. He was not aiming at a detached, professionally theological account such as that on which the authors who are mentioned below are engaged. Another point of difference is that our theologians are much preoccupied with a moral question of current concern, a question which had not arisen in Newman's time, namely that of the morality or otherwise of artificial contraception. In relation to this question, the *sensus fidelium* is often treated in such a way that its subjects are presented as being at variance with and separated from the magisterium, whereas for Newman the sense of the faithful bears unfailing testimony to hierarchical teaching as wax bears a seal. Another point is that it is often a question of what category is appropriate for the placing of the argument. Many of the modern theologians do not restrict the *sensus fidelium* to matters of faith and morals but extend it to touch temporal affairs and the realm of culture, even of politics. Newman had no thought of placing such matters in the sphere of the *sensus fidelium*; in *On Consulting* he is concerned with the Nicene dogma relating to the person of Jesus Christ. It seems inappropriate, on first thoughts, to treat these extra matters as being in the same category as articles of faith. The *sensus fidelium*, as it has been generally understood so far, has to do with infallibility; its sphere is to recognize with certainty whether a notion belongs within the body of Christian doctrine or not. Newman's exposition of the nature of the development of doctrine stipulates that a true development must exhibit 'unity of type' with the original idea, must retain its principles.[3]

There can be no ultimate certainty or absolute truth in the sphere of culture or social affairs. On the other hand, it is not altogether objectionable to hear the *sensus fidelium* being called in to give judgement on a matter which closely touches the domain of faith. A prime example here would be the liturgy. *The Oxford Declaration on Liturgy*, issued from there on 29 June 1996 by the Liturgy Forum of the Centre for Faith &

Culture, expressed the hope that 'any future liturgical reform would not be imposed on the faithful but would proceed, with the utmost caution and sensitivity to the *sensus fidelium*, from a thorough understanding of the organic nature of the liturgical traditions of the Church.'[4] In fact, a common complaint against the post-conciliar order of the Mass has been the absence of care for the religious sensibilities of the faithful or liturgical tradition.

As the title of this book shows, my intention in writing of the *sensus fidelium* is to make special reference to Newman's thought. It is for that very reason that I give some prominence to modern theological reflections on the subject. Newman, the master of the theology of doctrinal development, would be entirely averse to being thought to have uttered the last word on the *sensus fidelium*, or on any subject. On the other hand, though this body of work which is considered below may present the appearance of having genuinely moved on from Newman, yet much of it proves questionable on close examination. With regard to the Second Vatican Council in particular, these present-day reflections are offered in its name, yet at many points they are at variance with it or give what seems an unwarranted interpretation of its measures. The claim has been made for Newman that he is the father of Vatican II. Certainly, his writings contain, before their time, many of the great themes of the Council, as already remarked. In particular, his ecclesiology, Ian Ker maintains 'in important ways anticipates the great Constitution on the Church of the Second Vatican Council and ... remains highly relevant to some of the most sensitive theological problems of the postconciliar Church.'[5] Thus, Newman can offer a guiding and correcting hand where the Council's themes are overplayed or distorted, as is often the case. He will be called upon for that purpose here, but it will also be noted where Newman's thought is in accordance with what is said. I have in mind his theology in general, not merely that to be found in *On Consulting the Faithful*. My comments are sometimes made as the occasion arises but are mainly contained in my third chapter under the heading 'What Newman Would Say'. At the same time, where any statement appears strikingly out of tune with the Church's teaching, comment on it will be ventured even where no guidance from Newman is available.

The examples given below of the reflections of post-Vatican II theologians on the *sensus fidelium* are drawn from (a) two articles by John J. Burkhard of the Washington Theological Union, which appeared in *The Heythrop Journal*, entitled *Sensus Fidei: Theological Reflection Since Vatican II*, where Burkhard presents and examines the argumentation of several theologians who have written on the subject since the conclusion of the Council;[6] (b) an issue published in 1985 as a companion volume in the series *Concilium*, dedicated entirely to the theme of the laity and what is considered their 'teaching authority'.[7] (Burkhard also deals with some of the essays in this issue.) Burkhard remarks that he uses the term *sensus fidei* rather than *sensus* (or *consensus*) *fidelium*, the two terms (there are several others) most generally used by theologians writing on the subject. He chooses *sensus fidei* because it is the term used by the Council.[8]

In his articles, Burkhard examines chiefly what importance those theologians ascribe to the *sensus fidelium* in the life of the Church, its nature, who are its subjects and how it relates to the hierarchical magisterium. Some account of their reflections, based on

Burkhard's articles (except for those which I draw directly from the *Concilium* authors), now follows. Several of them are felt to have some quality which is reminiscent of Newman even though his name may not be mentioned; these will be considered first.

Essayists Who Reflect Newman's Thought

An essay by Leo Scheffczyk[9] is foremost among those which recall Newman. It is considered first, partly for that reason and partly because it points out several faults and deficiencies in the treatment of the *sensus fidelium* by theologians which the reader will then be able to recognize in some of the other essays.

Scheffczyk begins by drawing attention to the frequent misuse of the concept of the *sensus fidelium* by theologians today. Some of them employ it in such a way as to drive a wedge between the laity and the hierarchical magisterium. Thus, they use it to maintain the very opposite of what it is meant to convey. He points out two strands of inadequacy and under-evaluation. The one, borrowing from political theory, would present this spiritual faculty as an arrangement of checks and balances to prevent the abuse of power by any one group; the other would take it up as a useful device for imparting a greater sense of self-worth to the laity. Scheffczyk maintains that the true meaning of the *sensus fidelium* can only be seen in the mystery of the Church's nature as a communion of believers. The Church is to be understood as a sacrament where Christ and his Spirit ensure that interior oneness which expresses the mystery of the Church. He likens the relationship of the hierarchy and the body of believers to the organic reciprocity between the interior and exterior elements of a sacrament. He speaks of two distinct powers working together to bring about a higher order of unity, explaining that a differentiated unity is always a higher form of unity.

What is important in Scheffczyk's exposition is that these two functions exist only in relationship to each other and are never entirely separated. Each enjoys only a relatively independent meaning. Thus, he explains, the *sensus fidei* of all believers expresses the living tradition of the Church in day-to-day life and activity; this tradition is not derived from the hierarchical magisterium. The hierarchical office in its authoritative decisions and teachings represents the continuation of the mediatorship of Jesus Christ in word and proclamation. These authoritative acts and their content are not derived from the collective faith of believers but proceed directly from the Head of the Church, Jesus Christ himself. In terms of their relative independence, the *sensus fidelium* of the faithful receives direction, firmness and definiteness from the hierarchical magisterium and the magisterium derives concreteness and life from the body of the faithful.

Scheffczyk concludes by rejecting recourse to the notion of public opinion or to dominant trends in theology and Christian thought in general as expressing the *sensus fidelium*; such attitudes fail to do justice either to the *sensus fidelium* or to the nature of the Church as a sacrament.

Scheffczyk, in basing his treatment on the sacramentality of the Church, shows the inspiration of the opening section of *Lumen Gentium*: 'By her relationship with Christ, the Church is a kind of sacrament or sign of intimate union with God, and of the unity of all mankind.' In extending this sacramental analogy to the relationship between the body of believers and the hierarchy, he brings originality to the theme, but an originality without strangeness of doctrine.

The reason why this essay of Scheffczyk recalls Newman is that the latter's theology was deeply informed by 'the mystical or sacramental principle'. He wrote: 'Holy Church in her sacraments ... will remain, even to the end of the world, ... a symbol of those heavenly facts which fill eternity.'[10] Ian Ker observes: 'This profoundly sacramental vision meant that Newman never saw the sacraments of the Church apart from the larger sacramental reality, and particularly from the primordial sacrament, the Church herself.'[11] It seems fitting that Scheffczyk, a Newman scholar, should see his subject on this occasion, the *sensus fidelium*, which is also one of Newman's, in sacramental terms. He thereby brings two Newman themes together and in the process gives each of them a new aspect.

We come next to Harald Wagner in whose account of the *sensus fidelium* are also to be found several qualities which recall Newman.[12] For Wagner, as for Newman, the order of revelation is grounded in the Incarnation; both have a primary concept of the Church as the communion of those who have received the life-giving Spirit of Christ.

Wagner's analysis brings the *sensus fidelium* into very close relationship with the act of faith. His aim is to show this sense in terms, first, of the act of belief in the individual; next, how it can take ecclesial form; thirdly, how it is expressed in the life of the Church. In each case, he speaks of the *sensus fidelium*, identified as it is with the act of faith, as an exercise of infallibility.

Wagner maintains that there is a real identity between

the act of believing and the *sensus fidelium* in the believer. This sense is the elevation of a person's faculties, making him capable of receiving God, the object of belief. If the *sensus fidelium* is understood in terms of the act of belief itself, then any exercise of infallibility in the Church must be grounded in the infallibility of the very act of believing.

Wagner next considers the ecclesial form of this infallibility. The act of belief, though always an individual act, is enabled to take ecclesial form through the anointing of all believers by the Holy Spirit. The primary form of the Church's infallibility is not in extraordinary measures such as a papal or conciliar definition but in the ordinary day-to-day life of the Church. That is so because divine revelation takes place in the same manner. A deeper understanding of revelation can be of help towards explaining the exercise of infallibility in the Church. Just as the light of faith in the individual elevates his faculties and emotions, so revelation must be the raising of the communicative possibilities of human experience to the point where God's self-communication, that is, revelation, is enabled to be received by the whole body of believers, united as they are by the Spirit of God.

Lastly, Wagner points out another aspect of faith which can further help us to understand the nature of a concrete exercise of infallibility as the *consensus* of the whole Church. Faith, as St Paul says, comes 'by hearing'.[13] Each generation of Christians must bear the witness of the apostolic Church. In this task, the hierarchical magisterium must not hand on its witness as though it had the monopoly on how truth should be understood, or as though everything flowed directly from it, as first recipient, down to the faithful. He calls for a Christological understanding by means of which the incarnate Son of God would be seen as the Word of the Father uttered from all eternity. From this would follow the understanding that the Father's utterance is continued by the Son through the incarnate order of the faith itself and the Church's witness to it in the course of history. The Church is seen first and foremost as the whole *ecclesia credens*, the entire believing Church, which, following J. A. Möhler's perception, is understood as a community enlivened and pervaded by the Spirit of Christ. Wagner grants that the magisterium has its unique role which is none other than to present ever anew to the community of believers the event of Christ as witnessed to in the Scriptures. The teaching of the magisterium, when it *must* teach, should emerge from the experience of revelation by all believers in the ordinariness of human life and activity.

Like Wagner, Newman also, in *On Consulting the Faithful*, follows Möhler when explaining the *phronēma*, or instinct, in the mystical body, one of the aspects of the *sensus fidelium*. He quotes from Möhler's *Symbolique* in which he speaks of the Spirit of God governing and enlivening the Church and bringing about in man an 'eminently Christian' instinct.[14]

Of the theologians whose reflections are under consideration, Edmund J. Dobbin[15] is one of three only who speak of Newman by name (the other two being Jan Walgrave and Heinrich Fries). Dobbin examines the notion of the *sensus fidelium* by contrasting it with the *sensus fidei*. He, like Wagner, whose views we have just noted, sees the *sensus fidelium* in terms of what Newman called *phronēma*, a sort of instinct or collective discernment among the faithful. According to Newman, he explains, this sense of discernment constitutes a valid though different form of knowledge from logical reasoning. The *sensus fidei* Dobbin understands as a material criterion of what the Church believes. However, a static meaning, which he implies was once accorded to *sensus fidei*, he sees as no longer prevalent. It has given place to a dynamic search for consensus, best conveyed by the expression *sensus fidelium*; here, it is the concrete actions of believers which becomes the criterion of belief. Finally, Dobbin provides an outstanding example of that wedge driven between the hierarchical magisterium and the laity, as also the checks and balances arrangement, both of which Scheffczyk decries. Dobbin distinguishes between the *sensus fidelium*, which is the laity's charism of truth, from that of the hierarchical magisterium, which he calls the *sensus ecclesiae*, and calls for dialectical interaction between the two in order to secure authenticity of belief.

Dobbin attempts to apply the notion of *phronēma* in a way not at all sanctioned by Newman. For Dobbin, it opens up an avenue of thought which results in his moving away from what he calls the 'static' in the Church's beliefs in favour of a dynamic search for authenticity directed by what are observed to be the concrete actions of believers. That search, he suggests, is best conveyed by the expression *sensus fidelium*. Although Newman held that what came to be established as true dogma was that which obtained credence through the conscience and sensibility of the Christian body, he makes it plain that the approval of the faithful is not required in order to authenticate hierarchical teaching. Nor would Newman approve a formula for discerning the true from the false article of belief which depended upon the diminishing of the importance of the objective criterion in favour of 'the concrete actions of believers'. For him, right action and right belief go together. The place of the latter cannot be usurped by 'concrete actions'. No doubt Newman would consider that such actions may well be sinful.

The issue of *Concilium* referred to above has an address by Jan Walgrave[16] specifically on Newman's *On Consulting the Faithful*. Walgrave recalls how Newman had a persistent and dominant concern with the intellectual and religious education of the Catholic laity, with special emphasis on the need to cultivate in them the faculty of right and sound judgement. Newman wished for a laity that could think and speak for itself and participate in such discussion of ecclesiastical matters as touched on areas where they had special experience and competence. He did not contemplate the laity's joining in strictly scholarly theological disputes, though he wished them to have a developed knowledge of religion. This attitude was feared by the bishops whose great love was peace. They expected complete passivity from the laity. Newman's idea was that of wholeness, of organic unity and cooperation, yet he believed that tension and struggle were necessary to growth and life. For that, the Church needed the help of the laity because of their knowledge, judgement and practical skill in those provinces which belonged to their daily preoccupation. A continual collaboration in a spirit of mutual trust was required. Walgrave goes on to describe Newman's cast of mind which, he says, tended 'to keep always in view the wholeness or fullness of things and occurrences and never to lose sight of it in dealing with details' (p. 25). He always had a serene conviction that, in the end, truth would prevail. Walgrave mentions a distinction that Newman makes between the kingly, the prophetic and the pastoral offices of the Church and how he ascribes to the pastoral office the emotional needs of devotion; in that office, pastor and flock are united. Thus it is specially appropriate to consult the flock on doctrines which bear directly on devotional subjects such as the Immaculate Conception, on which they were, in fact, consulted.

Walgrave then comes to the heart of the matter he is discussing, that is, the nature of the *sensus fidelium* according to Newman, of which he gives a short, descriptive account. This will not be dwelt on just now as it is the subject of a later chapter of this book (Chapter 6). Walgrave ends his address by posing the question of how the testimony of the Catholic laity, so brought into prominence by Newman, can be related to what he calls the predicament of the contemporary Church. He sees the docility of the laity towards priestly teaching which existed in Newman's time, and which insulated them from the contrary influences of the non-Catholic world, as no longer obtaining. Through the all-pervading influence of the media, and of the non-Christian world about them, professed Catholics have become as worldly-minded as the rest of the populace. That being so, where are the faithful, Walgrave asks, whom the Church might wish to consult? He questions whether Newman's position on 'consulting the faithful' is still relevant and practicable.

Walgrave has no need for such doubts. Newman's position can be seen to be keenly relevant today as a much-needed corrective to the claims which are being made by theology that it is possible for an exercise of the prophetic office of the laity through the *sensus fidelium* to take the form of the rejection of magisterial teaching. Newman's exposition points to the witness of the laity, in union with their immediate pastors, to apostolic tradition. The question raised by Walgrave as to where, in today's world, a laity worthy of consultation can be found, I take up in Chapter 7; I consider there the matter of the present defective witness to apostolic doctrine and point to a remedy in the teaching of Pope John Paul II.

The post-conciliar theologian, William M. Thompson,[17] joins many of the rest in stressing the active character of the *sensus fidelium*. It is never to be thought of, he argues, as the purely passive reception of a truth imparted by the hierarchy to the faithful; its exercise is a true act of consensus between the faithful and the hierarchical magisterium. He insists, as would Newman, that the errors and excesses which have admittedly occurred in the Church do not detract from the ultimate indefectibility and infallibility of the Christian faith in her hands. Concerning the nature of the *sensus fidelium*, he rejects a view of it as a 'feeling' in the sense of something non-rational or a sort of 'sixth sense'. He explains it in terms of Aquinas's understanding that there is a preconceptual mode of knowing by which a person can grasp more than he can conceptualize or articulate. A similar explanation is offered by John W. Glaser whose views are discussed later in this chapter. Newman, in different language, also upholds the existence of such a mode of knowing; he calls it 'implicit' (as opposed to 'explicit') knowledge. Thompson places the action of the *sensus fidelium* within the scope of the action of the Spirit in the Church, basing his insistence on its active character on the fact of the direct empowering of the faithful by the Spirit. He emphasizes that the act of faith and its understanding as *sensus fidelium* are intrinsic to each other.

More Post-Vatican II Reflections

Having selected and discussed those essays which I see as recalling Newman's thought, I continue this account of post-conciliar reflections on the *sensus fidelium*. An early treatment of the subject came from Magnus Löhrer[18] who examined it in the context of the role of the whole Church as mediating divine revelation. The Church, being constituted in the divine gift of the truth of Christ, could never radically desert that truth. However, since God's truth is in the hands of human beings, it is exposed to the danger of limitation and sinfulness. Löhrer sees the resultant tension as being worked out in terms of kerygma and dogma, with the possibility of dogma obscuring and obstructing kerygma. There exists, he says, an underlying mutuality of action between the laity and the hierarchy through which the infallibility of the whole Church is expressed in human terms. The faithful are in need of the guidance and interpreting activity of the magisterium, but the magisterium in its turn needs the challenge and witness of the faithful. The insights of the faithful lead the hierarchy to a deeper understanding of the faith.

Although Löhrer's examination of the *sensus fidelium* is placed in the context of the whole Church as mediating divine revelation, his chief concern is seen to be with the specific contribution of the laity. For that purpose he designates them the 'Christian People' and awards them primacy of place in the Church's mission to mediate revelation afresh to each generation. He gives examples of the way in which this role is fulfilled: prayer and instruction in the family circle, or the activities of teachers, writers and artists who recognize the profane character of these activities and perform them as such. In these varied forms of mediating revelation, the Christian People bring the *sensus fidelium* to expression.

Löhrer attributes to the laity a unique grasp of the contemporary situation and its imperatives which makes them a *locus theologicus* for the hierarchy and for theologians. The Church's process of the mediating of revelation is not limited to the mere imparting of true propositions but is more a matter of a statement of the faith which must correspond to the historical situation. Löhrer regards the laity as being endowed with a special understanding of how the imperatives of a given situation are to be put into effect. What I suppose Löhrer to be referring to specifically when he speaks of 'the contemporary situation' is that in which the Church's teaching against contraception was the subject of much discussion; a reversal or modification of that teaching was hoped for, even expected, in several quarters. Löhrer was writing three years or so before the encyclical *Humanae Vitae*.

Löhrer appears as one of several of these authors who perceive the laity, because of their more practical involvement in life, as being in a position to correct or supplement the understanding of the hierarchy in certain situations. This would no doubt be true in many temporal areas but would not be so if Löhrer would show the way to a theologically justified rejection of papal moral teaching.

Löhrer speaks pointedly of the secular nature of the Christian lay people's calling. There is heard in this an echo of the Council's teaching on the laity to whom, it maintains, a 'secular quality is proper and special' and who 'by their very vocation seek the kingdom of God by engaging in temporal affairs and by ordering them according to the plan of God.'[19] Also, the emphasis Löhrer places on the laity's significance in their own generation anticipates a passage in Pope John Paul II's *Christifideles Laici*. There, Pope John Paul, having referred to the relevant sections of *Lumen Gentium*, concludes: 'The lay faithful's *position in the Church*, then, comes to be fundamentally defined by their *newness in the Christian life* and distinguished by their *secular character*'. (The italics are in the original.) The Pope explains this attribute of newness in the Christian life of the laity. He says that the Gospel images of salt, light and leaven are specifically applied to the lay faithful. Their involvement and participation in temporal affairs has a radical newness and unique character in that it has as its purpose the spreading of the Gospel that brings salvation.

There remains the question as to whether the lay activities Löhrer mentions can rightly be classified as an exercise of the *sensus fidelium*, though no doubt if performed in the Spirit of Christ they would be an exercise of the laity's prophetic office to which the *sensus fidelium* belongs. *Christifideles Laici* speaks of the various activities of the laity's daily life, if carried out in the Spirit, as becoming spiritual sacrifices acceptable to God through Jesus Christ.[20]

John W. Glaser, another writer whose reflections on the *sensus fidelium* appeared shortly after Vatican II,[21] deals with the topic without naming it as such. He is concerned with moral issues as met with and judged by the laity. He writes in the context of the debate on the morality of contraception which took place between 1963 and 1968, the years closest to the promulgation of *Humane Vitae*. He argues that the spontaneous moral judgements of loyal and faithful Catholics provide a theological datum for theologians and magisterium. He finds such judgement to be acknowledged in Catholic theological tradition. He calls upon Jacques Maritain and Karl Rahner to support his argument. According to Maritain, Aquinas held that there is a valid form of knowing which is not acquired through concepts and reasoning but through inclination or through sympathy, congeniality or connaturality.[22] A similar contrast between two forms of knowing is drawn by William M. Thompson as referred to earlier in this chapter, as also, in different phraseology, by Newman. As for Rahner, Glaser points out that he has argued for a distinction between two basic forms of knowing. There is on the one hand knowledge as conceptual, thematized and reflexive; on the other, knowledge as non-conceptual, non-discursive and non-reflexive. Both forms are valid; neither can rightfully claim the last word. Only fruitful interaction between the two forms can release each from the impasse which Glaser sees as having been reached. Presumably he is implying here that the conceptual and thematized form of knowledge is exercised by the hierarchical magisterium in its promotion of dogma, while the non-conceptual belongs to the general faithful. By the reaching of an impasse he seems to refer to the rejection on the part of many of the laity of magisterial teaching in *Humanae Vitae*.

An article by Jan Kerkhofs[23] examines the process of discernment which would permit the real exercise of the *sensus fidelium*. He cites with approval several instances where the hierarchical magisterium has paid close attention to the mind of the laity. Among his examples are the contact of the Brazilian hierarchy with the 'base communities'; the broad consultation carried out by the American hierarchy in connection with its pastoral letters on the economy and on questions of world peace and disarmament.

Kerkhofs goes on to consider public opinion in relation to the implementation of the *sensus fidelium* and concludes that it tends to be too inconclusive and not entirely reliable for the purpose. What is required to achieve consensus is true dialogue together with the availability of information. Where these two requirements have not been present, the result has been polarization of opinions. In order to avoid that situation the author calls for a process of communal discernment in the form of mixed groups at all levels: parish, diocese, nation, and world. A receptive attitude in all participants and real communication among them are essential if consensus is to be achieved. All have a part to play: 'prophetic voices', theologians from the various confessions and the hierarchy.

We find in Kerkhofs yet another writer on the *sensus fidelium* who would extend its meaning beyond the sphere of the discernment of true doctrine in matters of faith and morals; his attention is given also to areas of life where no final and objective certainty could ever be reached, whatever consensus were to be arrived at. This extension of meaning does not seem entirely inappropriate if it is the Christian communion one has in mind; no doubt it is to be expected that a people informed by the Spirit of Christ will bring special sensibilities to the assessment, for example, of the merits of political, economic or social theories and measures. However, Kerkhofs, in speaking of the process of communal discernment, would welcome, as well as the parish and diocese, 'nation' and 'world' to the conference.

A definition of the *sensus fidelium* is provided by Wolfgang Beinert, among whose reflections on the subject is an article written in 1971.[24] This sense is, he writes, a free charism of all members of the Church by which they come to an internal agreement as regards the object of faith and by virtue of which the Church in its totality acknowledges the object of belief (expressed in the *consensus fidei*) and confesses this belief in its daily life in constant fidelity to the hierarchical magisterium. He speaks of the *sensus fidelium* as a criterion of Christian truth, witness being borne in their different ways by both the laity and the hierarchy. The difference lies in the way the function is exercised, not in what is witnessed to. He puts forward an understanding of the hierarchy as representatives, but representatives in the biblical sense of being the personification and incorporation of the whole community. As a criterion of Christian truth the hierarchical magisterium has a certain priority because it interprets the truth critically and brings to bear a higher degree of reflection. On the other hand the *sensus fidelium* (that is, when it is being thought of as residing in the laity) is more complete in its witness to Christian truth and expresses it more concretely in the life of the Church. In that way the *sensus fidelium* is a unique criterion of knowledge of the faith. Beinert rejects that distinction which would present an active infallibility as belonging to the hierarchical magisterium and a passive infallibility as belonging to the laity; the receiving of truth and its confession by the laity is always something active. He refers to the imbalance created by the First Vatican

Council through its over-emphasis on papal infallibility, an emphasis corrected by Vatican II by its placing of the infallibility of the hierarchical magisterium in the setting of the infallibility of the whole Church. The earlier Council had, too, brought about an over-intellectualized attitude to revelation. The *sensus fidelium*, as well as being the charism of the whole Church, shows a living and active character that is in keeping with the Vatican II understanding of revelation in terms of a fellowship of the believer with God through the mediation of Christ the Saviour.

While Beinert sees the *sensus fidelium* as 'a free charism of all members of the Church' he considers that, as a unique criterion of Christian knowledge, it pertains to the laity and not to the hierarchy. He seems to base this on his view of the circumstances of our time. As he sees things, more and more issues faced by the Church today are of a practical rather than of a theoretical nature so that the magisterium is assisted in resolving them by the orientations offered by the laity.

Faith, says Beinert, is experiential and not merely an intellectual grasp of the content of faith. Moreover, it should not be seen in terms of the isolated individual but in terms of his membership of the Church. Beinert's concern with what is the historical situation of the Church, together with his ecclesial understanding of faith, led him to the conclusion that there is no subsistent truth, but only a truth that is possessed, maintained and professed by members of the Church. We shall see in due course (in Chapter 3) how Newman would contend that a truth can be 'possessed' without being openly 'professed'.

It is hard to reconcile that conclusion of Beinert's with what the Dogmatic Constitution on Divine Revelation

(*Dei Verbum*) of the Second Vatican Council has to say concerning the transmission of revelation. We read there:

> Now what was handed on by the apostles includes everything which contributes to the holiness of life, and the increase in faith of the People of God; and so the Church, in her teaching, life, and worship, perpetuates and hands on to all generations all that she herself is, all that she believes. (§8)

Of course it is the case that different areas of the truth fail to be emphasized and can even be obscured at various points during the Church's life on earth, to be brought into a stronger light at a later age. That is not the same as saying that there is no subsistent truth. Rather, it implies the opposite. Moreover, the conciliar document on Revelation speaks of God's choosing a people 'to whom He might entrust His promises' (§14). It seems safe to say that if divine revelation is a trust, then the Church, the new People of God, cannot at any time limit its responsibility to such truths as it is prepared specifically to acknowledge and bring into prominence at that time. It would be as if the trustees of an estate decided to allow parts of the trust property to lose their value in the mere pursuit of simplicity. As was indicated above, Newman would not endorse the trimming of the deposit of faith which Beinert proposes. However, Newman would agree with him on certain other points, particularly his welcome of the adjustments made by Vatican II to the understanding of infallibility and the Christian's personal relationship with God.

The author of the first article on the *sensus fidelium* to appear in French after Vatican II (with the exception of commentaries on conciliar teaching on the subject) was

J. M. R. Tillard, who, addressing a Colloquium on 'popular religion', dealt with that theme in the context of Christianity as composed of 'popular faith' and 'educated faith'.[25] The former, he suggests, is represented by the laity and the generality of the clergy, the latter by theologians and sometimes by the hierarchy. He thinks it possible to study the *sensus fidelium* today as the tension between the two types of faith. For example, he points out how the laity has largely rejected the magisterial teaching of *Humanae Vitae*, also how some have resisted the liturgical reforms which have taken place. As for the theologians, they have reservations concerning certain pious practices of the laity. (The rejection by the laity of *Humanae Vitae* does not seem to be a very good example of layman v. theologian tension since that rejection is very well supported among the most noted theologians, as the essays under consideration show.) He cites the appeal made to the belief of the people by Popes Pius IX and Pius XII in connection with the definition of the Marian dogmas of the Immaculate Conception (1854) and the Assumption (1950). He sees in that approach by the Popes an acknowledgement that the laity and their influence were considered a vital factor in the ongoing tradition of the Church.

Tillard propounds an understanding of the *sensus fidelium* as a *conspiratio* of laity, theologians and hierarchy which comes to expression today in the area of morality and the changed understanding of the human person. He speaks of orthopraxis as seeming to take precedence over orthodoxy. The concrete practices of the laity together with papal definitions as enlightened by the researches of theologians all contribute towards the determining of the faith of the Church. Like many of the other post-Vatican II theologians, Tillard is concerned that the Gospel shall not be identified with a purely intellectual content of truth but with personal 'interiorization', and decries the separation of faith as it is lived and experienced from some fixed understanding of the faith.

Tillard's paper was intended as a keynote address to which other speakers were expected to respond from their own areas of expertise. Fernand Dumont provided one of the responses,[26] calling for greater precision in Tillard's use of language. Moreover, in Dumont's view, the very notion of 'popular religion' is highly problematic. He speaks of a triad of elements to be taken into account which he designates 'faith', 'norm' (that is, dogmatic criteria) and 'expression'. He complains that 'expression' has been neglected. He uses this term to mean, not only the living out of the faith as a personal relationship between the believer and Jesus Christ, but also, and just as importantly, the cultural form in which it is framed. The imbalance against 'expression', the author claims, is what has brought about the rejection of the teaching of *Humanae Vitae* and the widespread disuse of the Sacrament of Penance. He concludes that the Church, in order to live an effectively Christian life today, must redress the imbalance by promoting and tolerating a broader base of cultural expression.

Dumont's observations provoke the comment that the practice of birth control by artificial means is certainly an expression of the culture of our times; but can the practice be Christianized by means of a greater emphasis on the fact that it exemplifies the temporal culture?

Newman would strongly support the contention that faith is more than a set of dogmas, as also the importance of a particular cultural setting and local mode of expression in relation to the faith. For example, he regarded as a serious misfortune the loss of the English element in the composition of the Church, no doubt having the Reformation in mind. Speaking of the restoration to England in 1850 of the Catholic hierarchy, he remarked that the English had good reason to be grateful to Pius IX who, 'by giving us a Church of our own ... has prepared the way for our own habits of mind, our own manner of reasoning, our own tastes, and our own virtues, finding a place and thereby a sanctification, in the Catholic Church.'[27] However, he would not have argued that 'norm' should ever yield pride of place to 'expression' or that the living out of one's faith should be set in opposition to dogma. He did not regard the various elements of the Christian life as being in competition.

Karl Rahner has two essays, from 1979 and 1984, which touch upon the subject of the *sensus fidelium*. In the first essay[28] he deals with the relationship between theology and popular religion (*Volksreligion*). He urges that theology nowadays needs to take more serious account of the proposals of popular religion since the *volk* have their own experiences, preoccupations and so on. They have their own insights into the faith which stem from the fact that their experience of revelation is closer than that of a reflexive form, such as theology, to the experience of the original addressees of revelation, who are mankind in general.

In the 1984 essay[29] Rahner speaks of a co-existence in today's Church between what the official Church teaches and a contrary belief. He avers that the factual belief of Christians is also a norm of faith since official faith statements have always been co-determined by the acceptance of those who hear them. Nowadays the widespread problems which the laity have with certain moral doctrines perhaps indicate that the Church should reflect further on these doctrines and introduce more nuances in its approach, perhaps even reformulations. Rahner concludes by recommending two steps which the 'official' Church ought to take if the faith is to be effectively preached in our time. First, it must try to reduce the great number and complexity of its beliefs to those which are central to the experience of faith today. Secondly, in order to achieve this, the 'official' Church must take into account the actual belief of the generality of believers. The response which Newman would make to Rahner's recommendations are included in my Chapter 3 under the sub-heading 'Doctrinal Selection'.

Schillebeeckx and Companions

The volume of *Concilium* issued in 1985,[30] which has been referred to earlier, was entitled *The Teaching Authority of Believers*. In an introduction headed 'The Legacy of the Council', the publication's editors, Johann Baptist Metz and Edward Schillebeeckx, describe its aim. It is to propound and substantiate in a theologically responsible manner a model in which believers are living subjects within the Church; that is to say, not mere passive recipients of Church doctrine.[31] The writers distinguish between the teaching office (belonging to the Pope and Bishops) and authority in teaching (which the volume urges should be acknowledged also in the laity). The contributions of Herbert Vorgrimler, Christian Duquoc and Heinrich Fries will be considered.

But first, something should be said of a relevant period

of post-conciliar history, a period of twenty-five years or so after the close of the Council in 1965, during which Hans Küng, Karl Rahner, Schillebeeckx and others of like mind, in the pages of the quarterly *Concilium* and elsewhere, dominated the Catholic scene and were held by many to be the interpreters par excellence of the Council. This was especially true of Rahner, two of whose essays were considered earlier in this chapter. His influence was enormous, one could say supreme, at this period of the Church. Schillebeeckx and Rahner had been *periti* at the Council. Yet, along with Hans Küng, they were to emerge in the years following as a magisterium of opposition to the lawful teaching authority of the Church.

Concilium, up to the early seventies, appeared as an organ of legitimate reform. Its adherents had included Yves Congar, the Swiss theologian Hans Urs von Balthasar and Joseph Ratzinger. By the early seventies it had become plain that the journal's policy was subversive; Balthasar, Ratzinger and the Jesuit theologian Fr Henri du Lubac, parted company with it and founded the rival organ *Communio*. They were to be joined by others of a reforming disposition but loyal to the Holy See. Balthasar, the intellectual equal of Rahner, now entered the field as his rival and chief of the orthodox interpreters of Vatican II.

In the issue of *Concilium* mentioned above, Herbert Vorgrimler, whose contribution is headed 'From *Sensus Fidei* to *Consensus Fidelium*',[32] recounts certain episodes in ecclesiastical history, pointing out that the growth of false teaching in the earliest days of the Church led to the view that office-bearers were necessary to guarantee the purity of the apostolic tradition of faith. The Gospel message was increasingly intellectualized by becoming the domain of theologians and bishops (who were themselves theologians for the most part). Thereby, the message was subjected to the narrowing effect of the dogmatic proposition. Despite this the Church Fathers were aware of the importance of the people's sense of faith. The agreement of all members of the Church, 'from the bishops down to the last member of the laity', as St Augustine put it,[33] was understood as the criterion of the genuineness of a tenet of the faith. Disputes in the Church, culminating in the Reformation in the first instance, resulted in the sense of the faith being associated with doctrinal infallibility. Vorgrimler goes on to cite the First Vatican Council as establishing the theological position that an active infallibility belonged to the popes and a passive infallibility to the Church as a whole. However, the distinction between active and passive infallibility was to give way to the Second Vatican Council's pronouncement in *Lumen Gentium* §12 that the supernatural appreciation of the faith belonged to the whole body of the faithful 'anointed as they are by the Holy One'.

Vorgrimler distinguishes between the *sensus fidei* and the *consensus fidelium*. In his view, the consensus of the faithful is the agreement which arises among believers as a result of the *sensus fidei*, the sense of faith; it is also the form of expression such agreement takes. Consensus is sought in a living and practical experience of the faith. He invokes Rahner's concept of mankind as the original addressee and transmitter of God's revelation. In connection with the *consensus fidelium*, we should consider the concrete performance of faith in terms of human life. The people are recipients of revelation in its most radical form. When they articulate their faith they have a real teaching authority which stems from their dignity as recipients of God's primary revelation. Matters such as the struggle for liberation and efforts towards peace enter into the picture as importantly as the tenets of the faith. The magisterium has a place in the work towards consensus but must take care to allow issues to arise from the felt needs of the laity and avoid raising complicated issues and principles of action. He refers to the particular understanding of natural law shown by magisterial instructions on birth control as an instance of departure from the simple, practical proclamation of Jesus and so unintelligible to the people. Thus, it is clear, he remarks, that a consensus on this matter in the form of an active acceptance by the people will not come about.

The term *Consensus* is used by Newman in his exposition but 'consensus' with him does not carry the meaning given to it by Vorgrimler. Newman would in all matters be concerned with the truth which for him was not born of consensus but of a consonance between intellect and objective reality. As do many of his fellow theologians, Vorgrimler sees 'consensus' as a situation to be aimed at; with Newman it is something which exists and is discovered in the common belief of hierarchy and people.

Vorgrimler claims a teaching authority for the laity. It is true that we read in *Lumen Gentium* that Christ continually fulfils his prophetic office 'not only through the hierarchy who teach in his name and with his authority, but also through the laity.'[34] But this statement would not justify the setting up of the laity's primeval endowments as addressees and transmitters of God's revelation in competition with the office-holders of the Church who teach in the name and with the authority of Christ. In order to fulfil his prophetic office in the laity the Lord 'made them his witnesses and gave them an understanding of the faith and the grace of speech (cf. Acts 2:17–18; Apoc. 19:10), so that the power of the gospel might shine forth in their daily social and family life.'[35] Not all of 'the concrete actions of the laity', a phrase to be met with in adverse commentaries on papal moral teaching, are worthy of the gospel. It becomes clear as Vorgrimler's essay progresses, apparently generalized though his comments are, that he is attempting to lend a theological justification to the laity's rejection of magisterial teaching on birth control.

Another contributor to this *Concilium* issue is Christian Duquoc[36] who seeks an active role for the laity in the matter of defining the faith of the Church. He begins by asserting that the traditional *modus operandi* of the Church, where the teaching authority is considered as belonging to the higher clergy in common with the Pope while the faithful give their assent to what is presented to them as the faith and take no active part, is being challenged. Many Catholics no longer accept that only the hierarchy has the real right to pronounce authoritatively on the fundamentals of their relations with Christ and God, or with their moral attitudes. He calls for the recognition and the defining of the authority of the faithful in discerning the faith, and for the institutionalization of that authority. He makes a distinction between the teaching office (exercised by the hierarchical magisterium) and authority in teaching which, he contends, is exercised by the laity also and is independent of any office. The *sensus fidei* is insufficient to express this authority since it is still interpreted as passive. Procedures not yet having been established for the laity to teach authoritatively, they do so *de facto* by means of public opinion. He complains that Vatican II's vision of a sharing of responsibility with the laity has not been implemented and that the people are still confined to a passive role in the doctrinal expression of the faith. He specifically mentions *Humanae Vitae* in connection with his arguments.

Duquoc speaks of the very practice of contraception by the laity as possessing authority. He claims that their opposition has proved at least that we have left behind the hierarchical model. He is too ready to claim this opposition as a mark of progress in the Church and to accord ecclesial worth and distinction to a practice which, it can just as well be argued, is a case of conforming to that of this present world.

In a *Concilium* article by Heinrich Fries entitled 'Is there a *Magisterium* of the Faithful?'[37] the author begins with the assertion that he regards the pronouncements of the Second Vatican Council as the most important principles relevant to his subject. He quotes the Council's declaration concerning the sense of the faith in the People of God as set out in *Lumen Gentium* §12. He adds a reference to §35 of that Constitution which declares that Christ, in continually fulfilling his prophetic office, does so not only through the hierarchy who teach in his name and with his authority but also through the laity. He sees in these passages, according as they do a dignity and importance to the People of God, as a shift from the earlier concept of the Church as having as its prime functional principle the vis-à-vis of clergy and laity. He considers that whoever shares in Christ's prophetic office, as do the laity, must do so in an active and vital way.

Fries points to Vatican II as having introduced an

understanding of revelation as the self-communication of God. Prior to the Council, he asserts, the concept of infallibility and its concentration in the magisterium was largely conditioned by the fact that divine revelation was viewed primarily as a disclosure of truths and teachings. Vatican II, he says, expressed both the infallibility of the People of God, the faithful, and the infallibility of Pope and bishops, but did not produce a perfect reconciliation between the two modes of infallibility. Nor was any association offered, he complains, between the testimony of the faith of the faithful in relation to the magisterium represented by the pope and bishops.

It is Fries himself who disjoins hierarchy and faithful, not the Council which fails to show how they are conjoined. It is clear from a disinterested reading of the conciliar texts that the body of the faithful has no teaching authority of its own independently of the hierarchical magisterium. All reconciliation which is required is expressed by *Lumen Gentium* §12 in these words:

> God's People ... clings without fail to the faith once delivered to the saints, ... penetrates it more deeply by accurate insights, and applies it more thoroughly to life. All this it does under the lead of a sacred teaching authority to which it loyally defers.

Fries' quotations from *Lumen Gentium* omit the reference to the loyal deference of the People to the *ecclesia docens*. Certainly to have included it would have been inimical to his argument.

Referring to the action of the Holy Spirit who inspires the whole body, the teaching body and the body of faith, Fries speaks of the arising of a twofold stream; or, he suggests the metaphor of a single light split into two beams. These are fine-sounding phrases but do not disguise the author's own intervention in driving a wedge, to revert to Scheffczyk's figure, between the laity and the hierarchical magisterium. Fries himself very appropriately chooses the word 'split' to describe the fracture he brings about (p. 86).

Later in his article Fries mentions briefly what he calls 'The continuing discussion of the problems raised in the encyclical *Humanae Vitae*.' He considers that situation to be the prime example of what happens when magisterial decisions are reached without sufficient consideration of 'what is living in the faith of the faithful.' He does well to call it the prime example since it is quite clear that support of the people's opposition to *Humanae Vitae* is the unstated object of his whole dissertation.

A section of Fries' essay, which gives examples from history of the significance of the activity of the faithful in questions of doctrine, contains comments on Newman's *On Consulting the Faithful*. These references need a careful comparison with Newman's text if the reader is not to be misled. For example, Fries states, as one of Newman's observations, that reference to the witness of the faithful is one of the requirements for a doctrinal proclamation. Newman gives instances of this practice: he does not name it as a requirement. Again, Fries says, too succinctly, that Newman observes that 'The *consensus fidelium* often replaces other theological sources.' This observation is filled out by Newman in a section in *On Consulting* where he explains why he came to lay stress on the *consensus fidelium*. Without Newman's fuller explanation, the mistaken impression might be gained that the *consensus fidelium* in Newman's treatment ousts other sources.

Fries wrote again on the subject of the *sensus fidelium*. In an essay of 1988,[38] not this time for *Concilium*, he raises again the question of relationship between the infallibility of the teaching office and that of the whole Church. He speaks of Vatican II as having restored the concept of infallibility to include the whole Church 'as well as a specific office of teaching' but expresses regret that the Council never explained how these two ministries of truth are related to one another. This lack of clarity, he claims, has contributed to the post-conciliar tensions in the Church.

An erroneous dichotomy has been introduced here in the use of the phrase 'as well as'. It is not, if Newman is to be believed, a question of two ministries of truth standing side by side and needing to establish what their relationship is to each other, or needing, as Fries goes on to suggest, the mediation of theologians between the hierarchical exercise of teaching and that of the laity. For Newman, 'the laity [are] but the reflection or echo of the clergy in matters of faith'; yet we see that seeming passivity to be productive when he adds the remark: 'yet there is something in the "pastorum et fidelium *conspiratio*", which is not in the pastors alone'. He refers to the history of the definition of the Immaculate Conception where, he says, 'Pope Pius has given us a pattern ... of the duty of considering the sentiments of the laity upon a point of tradition, in spite of whatever fullness of evidence the Bishops had already thrown upon it.'[39]

Regardless of the division between hierarchy and people which Fries himself attempts, he proceeds to warn against any understanding of the Church which seeks to divide it into a teaching Church and a learning Church; such an understanding, he contends, would show an erroneous and unhealthy view of the reality of the Church. Newman, it is true, does in his essay *On Consulting the Faithful* make an *ecclesia docens/dicens* distinction but there is nothing erroneous or unhealthy in this. What he makes is a distinction, not a division. As Jacques Maritain would explain, a distinction, to be truly a distinction, is made for the purpose of uniting the two things which are distinguished. A purported distinction which does not do this is a separation. Since Newman's language, as we have seen, unites the teaching Church and the learning Church, it is unobjectionable. To conclude, we go once more to *Lumen Gentium* where we read:

> For the distinction which the Lord made between sacred ministers and the rest of the People of God entails a unifying purpose, since pastors and the other faithful are bound to each other by a mutual need.[40]

Chapter Three

What Newman Would Say

I began my account of theological reflections on the *sensus fidelium* since the Second Vatican Council by pointing out how Newman was, in a sense, a precursor of that Council in that its measures could be seen as a fulfilment of many of the projections to be found in his writings. I expressed misgivings in many cases concerning the views of the post-conciliar writers whose essays I examined. I stated my intention of showing, chiefly under Newman's guidance, where I believed those writers where off course either in their purported following of the Council or in some general way.

What follows is not intended as a complete examination of Newman's thought in relation to that of the modern theologians, examples of whose writings have been given. It is just a matter of certain ideas of Newman's which came immediately to mind from time to time during the study of those writers and which are recalled here. The reader will remember references I made in the preceding chapter to several of Fr Ian Ker's writings on Newman. I shall have recourse to them again in the present chapter, as well as to other works of his on Newman, and this seems an appropriate moment to give an account of the author and his views, some of which he has recently expressed. Fr Ker was born in 1942 in India, his father having been a member of the Indian Civil Service, and was educated at Shrewsbury School and Balliol College, Oxford, where he obtained an MA degree in Classics. He is, like Newman, a convert to the Catholic faith. He was ordained to the priesthood in 1979 and is parish priest of Burford in Oxfordshire. He is a member of the Theology Faculty of Oxford University and Senior Research Fellow at St Benet's Hall, Oxford. Fr Ker is the author of a Newman biography of great distinction and of many other books on Newman and has edited many of his works. He has a Cambridge Ph.D. in English, a subject which he taught at York University during the years 1969–74. His writings include *The Catholic Revival in English Literature 1845–1961*. It was as a student of English literature that he first became 'fascinated', as he puts it, by Newman. Fr Ker is a supporter of the new ecclesial movements to which he has provided a 'Theological Introduction' for the Catholic Truth Society.

In the preface to his work *John Henry Newman* (the biography which I referred to above, first published in 1988) Fr Ker, who is the leading authority on Newman, wrote that his studies had led him to the conviction that Newman is to be numbered among the Doctors of the Church, while being aware that the Church would not declare him to be such unless he had first been canonized as a saint. Since then, in view of the progress of Newman's canonization cause, he has come to see the expectation he expressed in his preface as beginning to be realized. Fr Ker is an ardent champion of Newman. He seeks to promote a fuller appreciation of his importance in areas where he considers him to be generally undervalued, and is anxious to correct misunderstandings concerning him which have arisen of late. For example, Fr Ker believes there should be a reappraisal of

Newman's significance as a philosopher of religion, having principally in mind Newman's *Oxford University Sermons* on the subject of faith and reason and his *An Essay in Aid of a Gammar of Assent*. Also, in a chapter on Newman as 'Writer' in *The Achievement of John Henry Newman*, he points to an underestimation of certain aspects of his subject's merits in this field.

Fr Ker's biographical work, *John Henry Newman*, has recently been reissued with an 'Afterword' by the author to which he attaches much importance in that its purpose is to correct mistaken interpretations of matters relating to Newman's burial. He gives an explanation of the absence of remains in his coffin (discovered as the result of the customary order from the Congregation for Saints for exhumation for the purpose of public veneration) which caused raised eyebrows in some quarters. He refers also to a Victorian custom relating to burial with a friend and explains the particular circumstances which had led to Newman's instruction to be buried in the same grave as Ambrose St John, a fellow priest of the Birmingham Oratory. Fr Ker rebuts speculation, which became widespread in the press at the time when the facts of Newman's burial became generally known, that Newman's wish to be buried with St John indicated some kind of homosexual attachment.

Church: Communion of Persons and Institution

There will have been noticed among the post-Vatican II theologians a preponderant view of the Church as a communion. This presents a contrast to the Tridentine view which prevailed in Newman's time, and in our own prior to the Council, where the stress was upon the

Church as a juridical institution. It will have been noticed also that this stress upon the *communio* concept has been accompanied by some degree of mistrust and disparagement of 'the institutional Church'. Newman, contrary to the prevailing ecclesiology of his time, and more in accordance with the modern approach, held a concept of the Church as before all else a communion; he saw her as being first and foremost a communion of those persons who have been baptized by the Spirit into the union of Christ's body. He owed this approach to his study of the Fathers of the Church, in particular the Eastern Fathers,[1] a study through which he recovered for himself personally and took to heart doctrines and attitudes which had become overlooked during the centuries prior to the Council and had not been publicly and generally promoted until then. Examples of these are: The call to holiness of all members of the Church;[2] more awareness of the part played in salvation by the resurrection which had been neglected in the West where stress tended to be laid on the crucifixion alone;[3] a Trinitarian theology, again taken from the Eastern tradition, which showed a more careful differentiation between the three Divine Persons and a deeper understanding of their relationship.[4] Also, the importance which Newman, and the Council, attributed to the laity is well known. But his understanding of the nature of the Church as the communion of those baptized by the Spirit into union with Christ did not cause Newman to separate the mystical from the externally visible institution, or to minimize the hierarchical structure of the Church. He would reject the institution/communion of persons dichotomy, where the one restricts and deadens while the other exalts and enlivens, of which we have seen traces in today's theology; this in spite of the Council's injunction:

> But the society furnished with hierarchical agencies and the Mystical Body of Christ are not to be considered as two realities, nor are the visible assembly and the spiritual community, nor the earthly Church and the Church enriched with heavenly things. Rather they form one interlocked reality which is comprised of a divine and a human element.[5]

In preaching on this subject, Newman rejected the concept of an 'Invisible Church', a spiritual body, existing in the world separately from and independently of the 'Visible Church'. It was permissible to distinguish between the Church visible and the Church invisible so long as it was viewed as one, though under different aspects. The Church, he tells us, is 'a visible body, invested with, or ... existing in invisible privileges', for 'the Church would cease to be the Church did the Holy Spirit leave it', since 'its outward rites and forms are nourished and animated by the living power that dwells within it.'[6] Thus did the still Anglican Newman preach that view of the oneness of the Church which the Second Vatican Council saw the need to commend to us.

Newman on Magisterial Control over Dogma

Newman did not share the attitude to the magisterium and its control over dogma which is evident in much modern theological thought, both lay and, as we have seen, professional, that such control is somehow limiting to the fullness of life promised to the Christian. This kind of mistrust was particularly evident in the examples which have been given from the *Concilium* publication.

Newman's attitude to the Church's infallibility was one of trust and lively affirmation. He spoke of it as 'a supereminent prodigious power sent upon earth to encounter and master a giant evil'. He believed its effect was not constricting but that 'the energy of the human intellect ... thrives and is joyous, with a tough elastic strength, under the terrible blows of the divinely-fashioned weapon, and is never so much itself as when it has been lately overthrown.'[7] During the speech he made in reply to the *biglietto* of 12 May 1879 informing him that the Pope had elevated him to the College of Cardinals he declared: 'Against the anti-dogmatic principle I have set my whole mind.' This he had done as both Anglican and Catholic. Yet the spirituality of the Eastern Fathers in which he immersed himself kept him free of the over-philosophizing and rationalism of the West.[8]

Newman would strongly agree with that contemporary theology which insists that Christianity is a personal response, something to be lived, not just the acceptance of a number of propositions. He saw revelation, not as a set of propositions, but as historical events with the Incarnation at their centre. At one time he had begun to regard dogma as a necessary evil, but his attitude matured to the point where he saw doctrinal formulation as indispensable to personal faith. Creeds and dogmas are necessary, but only because the human mind cannot reflect except piecemeal upon the one idea which they are designed to express, As an Anglican, he did for a time share an opinion which seems nowadays to have become not uncommon among Catholic theologians, namely that the deposit of faith is cluttered with 'Roman additions'. As he proceeded towards his conversion he came to see the 'additions' as the result of a process 'by which the aspects of an idea are brought into consistency and form ... being the germination and maturation of some truth ... on a large mental field.'[9] He did not disparage adherence to dogma as somehow of inferior importance to the actual living of the Christian life, a tendency to be observed in the theologians (and the laity) of our time. His conviction was that 'The effectiveness of the Christian religion, its power of controlling and influencing our lives in the way God intends that it should, depends upon the fullness and correctness with which it is held.'[10] In his observation, 'the rovings of the intellect' demand formal statements concerning the object of worship.[11] If we are to love God, we must know him. 'Knowledge must ever precede the exercise of affections. The formula which embodies a dogma for the theologian readily suggests an object for the worshipper.'[12] Thus, Newman came to see doctrinal propositions as integral to faith itself. The Catholic faith rests in the Church as the organ of revelation and not simply in a number of set dogmas. 'The object of faith is not simply certain articles ... contained in dumb documents, but the whole word of God, explicit and implicit, as dispensed by his living Church.'[13] He deplored 'the common mistake of supposing that there is a contrariety and antagonism between dogmatic creed and vital religion.'[14]

Primary Revelation

His emphasis on the Church as the trustee of revelation did not mean that Newman overlooked or discarded the notion of a primary revelation such as Rahner, for example, has put before us. In his work, *The Arians of the Fourth Century* (1833) Newman, influenced in this respect, as in others, by the theology of the early Alexandrian Church, affirmed that 'There never was a time when God had not spoken to man and told him to a certain extent his duty.' Newman discerns 'a vague and uncertain family of religious truths, originally from God, but sojourning ... as pilgrims up and down the world, and discernible and separable from the corrupt legends with which they are mixed ...'[15] The idea that revelation could take place outside Christianity was strange to Newman's contemporaries and did not become generally accepted until the Second Vatican Council.

Doctrinal Selection

As for the suggestion, made by Rahner and Duquoc (Chapter 2), that the Church could profitably make a selection among her doctrines and discard such as are unpopular or not well understood, or because there are felt to be too many, Newman would have this to say: 'To object ... to the number of propositions ... is altogether to mistake their use; for their multiplication is not intended to enforce many things, but to express one.'[16] For Newman there was one, and only one, Christian message. He spoke of Catholic dogma as having evolved 'till the whole truth "self-balanced on its centre hung" part answering to part, one, absolute, integral and indissoluble, while the world lasts ... And this world of thought is the expansion of a few words, uttered, as if casually, by the fishermen of Galilee.'[17]

   What most strikes the student of Newman here is that to propose a reduction in the complexity and multiplicity of beliefs is to impugn the very notion of the development of doctrine as presented by him, for he explains such development as 'The process . . . by which the aspects of an idea [in the present case that of Christianity] are brought into consistency and form . . . being the germination and maturation of some truth or apparent truth on a large mental field.'[18] Doctrinal propositions 'imply each other, as being parts of one whole; so that to deny one is to deny all, and to invalidate one is to deface and destroy the view itself.'[19]

Still on the subject of Christian truth: we heard Beinert's opinion that for the Church on its pilgrim way there is no subsistent truth but only a truth that is 'possessed, maintained and professed' by members of the Church. Newman would say that there can be a truth which is possessed without being maintained or consciously professed. He held that a person, or the body of the faithful, can 'possess' a truth without, for the time being, 'professing' it, since it may lie hidden in the bosom of the Church and have not at a given point been called into the open by events or the passage of time, or even by its being denied. Newman's great argument concerning the development of doctrine was that a truth can be held 'implicitly'. He holds that 'naturally as the inward idea of the divine truth . . . passes into explicit form by the activity of our reflexive powers, still such an actual delineation is not essential to its genuineness and perfection.' Thus, a 'peasant may have such a true impression, yet be unable to give any intelligible account of it.' The impression made upon the mind may not even be recognized by the person possessing it. Similarly, in the mind of the Church, there may be impressions and judgements which are implicit for the time being. 'Even centuries might pass without the formal expression of a truth, which had been all along the secret life of millions of faithful souls.'[20] Newman shows here how rash it would be to attempt to reduce the number of beliefs to those which, in Rahner's phraseology, 'are central to the experience of the faith today.' Newman causes us to reflect what problems 'the official Church' (not an expression used by Newman) would meet with if it sought, in proclaiming the faith, 'to take into account [as Rahner would have it do] the content and the emphases of the factual belief of the generality of believers', (this on the footing that many of them have discarded doctrines held by previous generations).

Rahner maintains that there has been no time when the faith as proclaimed by the Church's official witness was not co-determined by the acceptance of those who heard the message. On the subject of reception, Newman would not speak as though the hearer's failure in any instance to take to himself the word of God would in any way invalidate it as the objective truth. Speaking of the pronouncements of an infallible Pope or Council, he says: 'I have never been able to see myself that the ultimate decision rests with any but the general Catholic intelligence.'[21] However, this does not mean, as Newman was careful to emphasize later when discussing the Catholic conscience vis-à-vis a papal decision, that the 'subsequent reception' actually entered into the 'necessary conditions' of a dogmatic decision. He had simply meant that the whole Church ratified a definition as 'authentic'.[22]

On this matter of reception of a dogma the Council shows us, in *Lumen Gentium* §12, that it is a case of the whole Church being at one in belief. The infallibility in teaching is met by a corresponding infallibility in believing. Aidan Nichols, invoking St Augustine, puts it in this way: '[S]ince all Christians are illuminated by Christ the internal teacher, they are enabled not just to receive the truth but "to make approval of that doctrine, to receive that doctrine as the truth."'[23]

Newman points out that an infallible decision of Pope or Council still, as time goes on, receives the attention of theologians who 'settle the force of the wording of the dogma, just as the courts of law solve the meaning and bearing of Acts of Parliament.'[24] That he should use such a simile shows that he cannot mean to say that the theologians may then set about searching for a way, theologically justifiable in their view, of rejecting papal or conciliar teaching. Newman does, it is true, set much store by a process which he calls 'the principle of minimizing' and which he regards as central to the interpretation of dogmatic statements.[25] But such efforts on the part of theologians are seen by him as working towards acceptance, not rejection, of official teaching. For example, on the subject of the doctrine *extra ecclesiam nulla salus* (there is no salvation outside the Church), among Newman's observations was that it did not apply to a person in invincible ignorance[26] and that it was 'possible to belong to the soul of the Church without belonging to the body.'[27] The object of this minimizing attention on the part of the theologians is, in Newman's teaching, 'to make [the doctrine] as tolerable as possible, and the least of a temptation, to self-willed, independent, or wrongly educated minds.'[28] 'Minimizing' is not, one may think, an altogether appropriate word, since the effect of the exercise according to Newman is eventually to see the initially unacceptable dogma assimilated and harmonized into the wider context of Catholic belief.[29] In fact the result is enrichment rather than diminution.

Newman employs, very aptly, a legal analogy to describe the position of the hierarchical magisterium with regard to revealed truth.

> [God] formed a society of men to be its [the Gospel's] home, its instrument and its guarantee [so that the] rulers of the Association are the legal trustees, so to say, of the sacred truths which He spoke to the Apostles by word of mouth.[30]

This figure of trustees deserves to be considered before we begin to urge that the magisterium should trim, change or do away with any item of the deposit of faith. Reflection on Newman's trustee simile shows how impossible it would be for the magisterium to play fast and loose with what, pursuing the simile, we may call the trust property; especially could they not justify the putting of that property at risk by the argument that they were attempting to make it more profitable. Newman never showed impatience with the Church, or sought to dictate to her, saying how she must without delay do this, or do that, if she is to be effective, in the way we have seen with Rahner, for example, and Duquoc. The Church for him is the dispenser of truth, and truth is the daughter of time. The truth is certain to emerge but we may have to wait for it. He believed strongly that God wishes events to happen at one time rather than another.[31]

Corruption in the Church

However, Newman was far from taking a starry-eyed view of the Church. He was very conscious of corruption in it. He was much afflicted personally by the runaway ultramontanism with its obstruction of the least freedom of thought and expression prevalent in his day, 'which exalts opinions into dogmas and has it principally at heart to destroy every school of thought but its own.'[32] At the same time, as theologian, he took a serene view of corruptions, considering them to be a sign of life, as inseparable from a living Church. 'Things that do not admit of abuse have very little life in them.'[33] It was the quality of life which Newman saw as an especial note of the Church.[34] In his Third Preface of 1877 to *The Via Media* (1837) in which he studied the problem of corruption in a profound theological manner, he considered how corruption stemmed from the difficulties attendant upon the existence and exercise of the triple office of the Church, that is, 'teaching, rule and sacred ministry' for 'Christianity . . . is at once a philosophy, a political power, and a religious rite.' He has in mind, of course, the Christian offices of prophet, king and priest. The problem of exercising these three very different functions 'supplies the staple of those energetic charges and vivid pictures of the inconsistency, double-dealing, and deceit of the Church of Rome, as found in protestant writings'[35] (among which he includes his own *Via Media*, written before his conversion). As an Anglican he had thought at first that corruptions came from theology, that is to say, he saw certain Catholic dogmas which had emerged since patristic times as unwarrantable Romish accretions; later, he came to believe that corruptions had a popular or else a political origin; popular in the area, for example, of superstitious practices, political in a faulty manner, perhaps, of the exercise of the ruling office.[36]

Popular and Educated Faith

We have seen how Tillard and Rahner wrote on this subject (Chapter 2). Newman saw popular and educated faith in terms of theology keeping a watch over the piety of the faithful at large in order to guard it against excesses and to modify and purify pious practices. Sometimes the hierarchy will take the part of the people against theology.[37] An endorsement of this perception is to be found in Tillard's essay; he sees in the pious practices of the laity in relation to Marian belief, practices not officially endorsed though tolerated by the hierarchy, but not altogether approved by theologians, a victory of 'popular faith' over 'educated faith'. This victory he speaks of came with the promulgation of the dogmas of the Immaculate Conception and the Assumption in 1854 and 1950.

Newman remarks that the Church allows much more freedom in devotion than in theology.[38] What is alien to the genius of the Church, because of her tenderness for souls, are sudden and violent changes in thought, 'for unlearned and narrow-minded men get unsettled and miserable.' However, theology has an important role in preparing the Church for change and accustoming people's minds to the idea.[39] Newman traces the distinction between the Church's attitude to the excesses of popular religion on the one hand and theological error on the other to the Gospel itself, citing the case of the woman who touched the hem of Jesus' garment in the hope that her haemorrhage would be cured. Jesus did not rebuke her for her superstition but healed her because of her faith. Newman argues that the Gospels show that 'the idolatry of ignorance' is not classed as on a level with other idolatries, that of money, for example. Jesus, says Newman, constantly insisted on the necessity of faith but nowhere did he warn against the dangers of superstition.[40]

There is an important strand in Newman's thought which can be placed under this heading of 'Popular and educated faith' on the ground that he shows (in those of his writings which deal with the attainment, or way towards religious faith, rather than with its exercise), not how the learned and the educated mind work differently from each other but how they work in the same way. The works in question are *An Essay on the Grammar of Assent* and his collection of *Oxford University Sermons* which presaged the *Grammar*. Ian Ker, writing on 'Newman the Philosopher', claims Newman's perceptions of the working of the human mind to be egalitarian and 'democratic' and thus as calling in question the charge of elitism sometimes made against Newman.[41] Newman was able to form this view by means of the distinction he made between 'implicit' and 'explicit' reason, a distinction to which we have already had occasion to refer in connection with the development of doctrine. Newman explained it as the difference between 'the more simple faculties and operations of the mind, and that process of analyzing and describing them which takes place upon reflection.' He considered that all people, lettered and unlettered, reason in the same way, that is, not by rule but by an inward faculty.[42] Ian Ker explains how Newman rejected the received understanding of reason which had obtained since the seventeenth century where philosophers had followed either the rationalism of Descartes or the empiricism of Locke; that is to say, they considered that knowledge was either deduced from logical a priori truths or derived a posteriori from sense experience by induction, or from both.[43] Newman argues that we act on antecedent probabilities in reasoning, claiming that 'antecedent probability is the great instrument of conviction in religious (nay in all) matters' and that 'It is how you convert factory girls as well as philosophers.'[44] He defines faith as 'the reasoning of a religious mind, or of what Scripture calls "a right and renewed heart", which acts upon a presumption rather than evidence, which speculates and ventures on the future when it cannot make sure of it.' He maintains that 'we must assume something to prove anything, and can gain nothing without a venture.'[45] The measure of probability necessary for conviction varies with the individual mind.[46]

In 'The Theory of Developments in Religious Doctrine', one of his Oxford University sermons, Newman brings together the faith of the learned and the unlearned Christian when he points out how the Evangelists made the Blessed Virgin Mary the pattern of faith: 'Mary's faith did not end in a mere acquiescence in Divine providences and revelations ... she "pondered" them', and, [regarding her Son's remarks on being found in the Temple] 'His mother kept all these sayings in her heart.' Newman then refers to the faith which anticipated the miracle at Cana, and goes on:

> Thus St Mary is our pattern of Faith, both in the reception and in the study of Divine Truth. She does not think it enough to accept, she dwells upon it ... not enough to assent, she develops it; not enough to submit the Reason, she reasons upon it ... And thus she symbolizes to us, not only the faith of the unlearned, but of the doctors of the Church also, who have to investigate and weigh, and define, as well as to profess the Gospel.[47]

Unlike some of our contemporary theologians, Newman is not impatient or distrustful of doctrinal truth in the hands of the 'teaching Church', nor does he ever see its imposition as unwarrantable or as subject to revision by the laity. What he did see as a source of difficulty was the Church's legitimate authority in 'secular matters which bear upon religion', that is, in making disciplinary rather than doctrinal judgements. He acknowledged that legitimate power was sometimes harshly used, but it does not follow that 'the substance of the acts of the ruling power is not right and expedient, because its manner may have been faulty.'[48]

The Importance of Obedience

In both spheres, disciplinary and doctrinal, Newman strongly urged obedience to authority. There are to be found in his writings two considerations which made him so certain that obedience was all-important. These, in someone who, on the one hand suffered himself from heavy-handed ecclesiastical discipline and, on the other, was an initiator, and still looked to as the masterly exponent, of the notion of doctrinal development, should surely be heeded. First, he held the strong conviction that there was a right and a wrong time for 'a reformation of an abuse, or the fuller development of a doctrine, or the adoption of a particular policy'.[49] He wrote in a letter to his friend, Henry Wilberforce: 'What I may aim at may be real and good, but it may be God's will it should be done a hundred years later.'[50] In Newman's own case, it is that very thing which has happened in the measures of the Second Vatican Council. He considers that a person who pushes these changes at an unseasonable time and in defiance of authority:

[S]poils a good work in his own century, in order that another man, as yet unborn, may not have an opportunity of bringing it happily to perfection in the next. He may seem to the world to be nothing else than a bold champion for the truth and a martyr to free opinion, when he is just one of those persons whom the competent authority ought to silence.[51]

Secondly, Newman, in the matter of obedience, was very conscious of the power of the thin end of the wedge. Writing on the subject of Wycliffe and reform, he concedes that there were many things that did need reform but points out how Wycliffe took to acting wrongly in its pursuit:

Then, as all would-be reformers, he takes upon him duties which are not his – and gets into a false position. From attacking ecclesiastical abuses, he goes on to attack received doctrine ... His career is like that of many others – Scripture says that 'rebellion is like witchcraft and idolatry;' in other words, that men begin with disobedience and end with spiritual blindness.

He cites also the example of Milton who, he says, began with extreme revolutionary opinions and ended with renouncing the divinity of Christ and the cardinal doctrines connected with it.[52]

Newman on Theologians

The impression must not be given that Newman was opposed to freedom of thought and expression on the part of theologians. In *Lectures on the Prophetical Office*, written by him as an Anglican, he had made what he later saw as a mistake in blaming the corruptions of the Church on theology. In correcting this mistake by means of his 1876 Preface to *The Via Media*, after he had seen that the corruptions 'bear on their face the marks of having a popular or political origin', he points out that 'theology, so far from encouraging them, has restrained and corrected such extravagances as have been committed, through human infirmity, in exercise of the regal and sacerdotal powers.' He adds that religion is 'never in greater danger than when, in consequence of national or international troubles, the Schools of theology have been broken up and ceased to be.' He gives this reason:

> Theology is the fundamental and regulating principle of the whole Church system. It is commensurate with Revelation, and Revelation is the initial and central idea of Christianity. It is the subject-matter, the formal cause, the expression of the Prophetical Office, and, as being such, has created both the Regal Office and the Sacerdotal. And it has in a certain sense a power of jurisdiction over these offices, as being its own creations, theologians being ever in request and in employment in keeping within bounds both the political and popular elements in the Church's constitution – elements which are far more congenial than itself to the human mind, are far more liable to excess and corruption . . .[53]

Newman agreed with the view, sometimes expressed by the Church's critics, that it was always individuals, and not the Holy See, that had taken the initiative and acted as leader in theological enquiry; he was content with that state of affairs.[54] He admired the way in which, throughout the Church's history, authority had been slow to interfere with theological scholarship (though not in his own time where authority made signs of assent or dissent to each sentence as it was uttered). That erstwhile restraint made for courage in theologians.[55] Yet he held the strong conviction that the Church's authority, when she did see fit to exercise it, had an invigorating rather than an enervating effect upon the Catholic intellect. Writing of the conflict between infallibility and reason, he claims that:

> The energy of the human intellect 'does from opposition grow'; it thrives and is joyous, with a tough elastic strength, under the terrible blows of the divinely fashioned weapon, and is never so much itself as when it has lately been overthrown.

He believed that the conflict between authority and private judgement, 'that awful, never-dying duel' [was] 'necessary for the very life of religion' and 'should be incessantly carried on.'[56] This calls for reconciliation with his insistence on the need for submission to authority. Newman is given to abrupt shifts of perspective which seem to stem from his gift for seeing what could be said for each of two differing opinions or viewpoints. Because of his historical knowledge and perspective he was aware that heresy could be a matter of bad timing. The Church itself has originated nothing; it was individuals who had taken the initiative. The best early exposition of ideas which were to form the theology of the West came from the African Church, and this to a large extent from heterodox theologians such as Tertullian, Origen and Eusebius. As Newman tells us: 'Heretical questionings have been transmuted by the living power of the Church into salutary truths.' Ecclesiastical authority has been guided in its decisions 'by the commanding genius of individuals, sometimes young and inferior of rank.' Newman insists that history shows us that, in spite of abuses, ecclesiastical authority has been 'mainly in the right and that those whom they were hard upon were mainly in the wrong.' He believed in the value of conflict between the human intellect and authority because each was sustained by the other. He says: 'Every exercise of Infallibility is brought out into act by an intense and varied operation of the Reason, both as its ally and its opponent, and provokes again, when it has done its work, a reaction of Reason against it.' Newman defends the Church's authority against an attitude which would see humanity as being hopelessly weighed down by it; he uses these stirring words:

> Catholic Christendom is no simple exhibition of religious absolutism but presents a continuous picture of Authority and Private Judgement alternately advancing and retreating as the ebb and flow of the tide; – it is a vast assemblage of human beings with wilful intellects and wild passions, brought together into one by the beauty and the Majesty of a Superhuman Power . . .[57]

The process which is urged in many of the post-Vatican II essays we have considered above is one of compromise, of the hammering out of a solution to conflict or argument which takes account of all opinions. The solution to such a process tends to be an artificial 'statement' which fails to a greater or lesser extent to meet reality, as has happened with certain ecumenical initiatives in our time. Newman, on the other hand, being interested in the truth, not in the emergence of some agreed verbal construct, did not believe that truth was attained by the route of compromise. He believed that truth is indeed attained in the arena where opposites are in conflict, but that is because, as Ian Ker observes, that very conflict 'forces the crucial shift of perspective that allows the dilemma to be seen in a new light and so to be resolved.'[58] Newman's idea was one of wholeness and organic unity combined with the idea of polarity, tension and conflict. These he regarded as the necessary conditions of life, and for him the leading mark of the Church was life.[59]

Chapter Four

History of the *Sensus Fidelium*

Scriptural Origins

The *sensus fidelium* belongs to the prophetic charism which is present among God's people and is anticipated in Scripture, both Old Testament and New, by passages which deal with the gift of prophecy. The key texts are of two kinds. Of one kind are those which promise or depict a more universal outpouring of the charisms of priesthood, kingship and prophecy. That is to say, the people are given to participate in the charisms or offices originally bestowed upon individuals. That general endowment, however, is already implicit in the fact that the Old Testament priests, kings and prophets are given these offices not for the sake of the holders but on behalf of the people. The great problem of spirituality is whether or not the people as a whole can ever come to participate in the spirit of royal and prophetic priesthood. The relevant texts, for example Jeremiah 31, Isaiah 54, Joel 2, all reflect past failures and promise success in the future (*eschaton*) through grace. As a result, history becomes a history of salvation. Further key texts are those which anticipate an extension of the meaning of the People of God. The Christian message not only considers that the *eschaton* has in some sense already happened (grace having been given through the Paschal Mystery) but that it has also been extended to the gentiles, the 'nations', to whom is also extended membership of the People of God. In that way there are fulfilled and developed the universalist concepts in the Old Testament, for example: 'The sceptre shall not be taken away from Juda . . . till he come that is to be sent: and he shall be the expectation of nations' (Gen. 49:10). Then, from Isaiah: '[T]he nations that knew not thee shall run to thee, because of the Lord thy God, and for the Holy One of Israel' (Isa. 55:5).[1]

The Old Testament foretells a new, messianic dispensation, doing so by means of promises of knowledge and inwardness addressed to the new people as a whole. The old texts are all repeated or evoked in the New Testament and presented as being fulfilled in the faithful people of Jesus Christ. Among the chief texts are:

> Behold the days shall come, saith the Lord, and I will make a new covenant with the house of Israel and with the house of Juda. I will give my law in their bowels and I will write it in their heart: and I will be their God, and they shall be my people. And they shall teach no more every man his neighbour, and every man his brother, saying: Know the Lord. For all shall know me from the least of them even to the greatest . . . (Jer. 31:31, 33-4). Cf. Heb. 8:8-12. [I] will pour out my spirit upon all flesh: and your sons and your daughters shall prophesy: your old men shall dream dreams, and your young men shall see visions. Moreover upon my servants and handmaids in those days I will pour forth my spirit (Joel 2:28-9). Cf. Acts 2:17ff.

The Lord himself repeated these promises to the apostles at the Last Supper with the whole Church in view: 'And I will ask the Father; and he shall give you another Paraclete, that he may abide with you for ever; The Spirit of truth, whom the world cannot receive, because it seeth him not, nor knoweth him. But you shall know him; because he shall abide with you and shall be in you' (John 14:16, 17). 'But when the Spirit of truth is come, he will teach you all truth' (John 16:13). Apostolic writings bear witness to the fulfilment of these prophecies in the faithful. All know the things of faith (1 John 2:20, 27); all are taught by God (1 Thess. 4:9). St John reminds his 'little children': '[Y]ou have the unction from the Holy One and know all things.' There was no need for any man to teach them (1 John 2:20, 27).[2]

Christ instituted the prophesied 'new covenant', that is, the New Testament, in his blood by calling together a people, with himself as its head, made up of both Jew and gentile whom he united in the Spirit to become the new People of God. Those who believe in Christ, who are reborn from water and the Holy Spirit (John 3:5-6), are finally established as 'a chosen race, a royal priesthood, a holy nation, a purchased people ... You who in times past were not a people; but are now the people of God' (1 Pet. 2:9-10).

'Prophecy' and the *Sensus Fidelium*

Through their baptism the faithful participate in the threefold mission of Christ as priest, prophet and king.[3] The prophetic office in the Church is equivalent to magisterium or the teaching function. However, the term 'prophecy' as applied to the messianic office of prophet has a wider and less precise meaning. It embraces all activities of knowledge and expression which do not come under the heading of magisterium or teaching. Understood in its widest sense, it includes all the work of the Holy Spirit in the Church whereby she knows God and his purpose of grace and makes them known to others.[4]

Christ's faithful are his flock and he their Shepherd; yet understanding is not exclusive to the Shepherd. The flock are united to him through his Spirit and are endowed by the same Spirit with understanding and discernment.[5] Christians can be said to be 'taught of the Lord' because they are illuminated by Christ the internal teacher; by that inward light they are enabled not only to receive doctrinal truth but 'to make approval of that doctrine, to receive that doctrine as the truth.'[6]

Although they have that inward light, Christians are not given knowledge of God and His purpose in a disorderly or haphazard manner and regardless of the magisterium and the organization of the Church. Congar explains:

> [A]ll the faithful receive light and are active, but this is *through the knowledge received from the apostolic word and set in order by the apostolic authority*. Their light and their activity are in no way equivalent to a revelation, to independent and direct knowledge; they are simply a living, personal understanding of the revelation made to and received from the Apostles ...[7] (The italics are Congar's.)

Since the *sensus fidelium*, a charism of the whole flock of Christ together, is intrinsic to faith it seems it must be no less an endowment of the individual disciple who may be called upon to bear witness to Christ *contra mundum*. This individual might be St Athanasius, or he might be, in Newman's words, 'the humblest and meanest among Christians' defending the faith according to his intellectual capacity.

The *Sensus Fidelium* in the Church Fathers

Several texts of the Church Fathers contain recognizable allusions to the *sensus fidelium* though the expression itself is not used. Congar points out that these texts fall under two main lines of argument.[8] One of them maintains that the truth of a doctrine is held to be testified to by reason of its representing the faith of the whole Christian people on the matter, the other by its being reflected in communal practice. The Fathers tend to a kind of *reduction ad absurdum* argument when claiming that a belief universally held must be true. Examples from the first category include Tertullian who asks: 'Equid verissimile est ut tot et tantae in unam fidem erraverint?' (Is it likely that so many would have erred in holding to one and the same faith?) By the expression 'so many' Tertullian was referring to the apostles who would have been wrong in their teaching, 'all the Churches', the vicar of Christ who would have neglected his office and so forth.[9] On similar lines, St Gregory Nazianzen is quoted as declaring that if the Catholic faith on the Incarnation and Christ's divinity is not true, then 'our faith is vain, the martyrs died in vain, bishops have ruled their people in vain ...'[10] and St Basil protests against a deviant believer: 'Scorning the conviction of the multitude that glorifies the Holy Spirit [as God] he professes to follow the teaching of the saints ...'[11]

The second category mentioned, that is, argument for a doctrine from common practice and belief, includes a text from St Epiphanius who asks, 'Has anyone at any time ever dared to call on the name of blessed Mary without adding "the virgin"? ...' such practice being regarded as confirmation of the dogma of the virginal conception of

Jesus.[12] St Nicephorus in his turn argued against the iconoclastic emperors from 'the faith of the people, their spontaneous inward inclination, the eagerness, the religious care with which [the images] are treated, the old and continuous custom handed on in the Church...'[13] St Augustine, among many texts, appeals to the Church's practice, sometimes calling it *dogma populare*, on four points in particular, these being: That there is no need to rebaptize repentant heretics;[14] the necessity of grace, evidenced by the meaning given by the faithful to prayer;[15] the canonicity of biblical books, such as Wisdom, which are listened to 'by all Christians, from the bishops even to the last members of the lay faithful ... with the veneration proper to divine authority';[16] the necessity and efficacy of baptism for salvation.[17]

The *Sensus Fidelium* in the Church Councils

The first of the Church's general Councils to be held after the beginning of the Reformation was that of Trent. Because of a long succession of hindrances it did not assemble until 1545, that is to say twenty-eight years after Martin Luther's proposal at Wittenberg of a debate on the indulgence system and other Catholic practices which he considered to stem from a misconception of the means of salvation. The Council closed in 1563. Its purpose was to discuss and reaffirm the whole body of Catholic teaching in the light of Protestant criticism. In presenting the Church's common tradition, the Council called upon the *sensus Ecclesiae* on several occasions. For instance, it spoke of those who deny Christ's real presence in the Eucharist as being 'against the universal sense of the Church'.[18]

The First Vatican Council met in the years 1869–70 during the papacy of Pius IX which saw the downfall of the public status of Catholicism in the countries of Europe, the loss of the papal states and the end of the papacy as a temporal power. However, the reign of Pius was a time of spiritual renewal in the Church. For instance, the revival of the Benedictine and Dominican orders came about in those years; St Jean Marie Vianney, the Curé of Ars, who was to become the patron of parish priests, lived at that time, as did St Bernadette Soubirous, the visionary of Lourdes. Vatican I re-emphasized the spiritual reality of the papal office. It defined anew the doctrine of the primacy of Peter among the apostles and reaffirmed the primacy and infallibility of the Pope as Peter's successor. It had set out to consider the matter of the Church's infallibility and had prepared a draft document on the subject which spoke of the Church's incapability of error as characterizing 'as much the universality of the faithful as the universality of the bishops', since what all the faithful hold as of faith is necessarily true. Owing to the Council's decision to proceed first with the consideration of papal infallibility, and the suspension of the Council on the outbreak of the Franco-Prussian war, the draft document referred to was never voted on or promulgated. It fell to the Second Vatican Council a century later to formulate the doctrine of the infallibility of the whole Church.

Pope John XXIII's announcement of his intention to convoke what came to be known as the Second Vatican Council (1962–65) was a complete surprise. The Council's keynote was *aggiornamento*, bringing up-to-date. Its central aim was to present in efficacious ways the truths of the Gospel to the people of the age. In an opening message to humanity the Fathers of the Council, in the words of Fr Walter M. Abbott, SJ, looked to 'renewal of the Catholic Church, to compassionate dialogue with modern men, to peace, to social justice, to whatever concerns the dignity of man and the unity of mankind.' In particular, the Council sought to promote unity among Christians. The opening message shows awareness of the world's problems; it emphasizes the quest for a community of peoples, the motivation that comes from Christ's love, the need for cooperation with all men of goodwill.[19] The Council was dominated by a pastoral tone which had been set by Pope John. It is often claimed that it was entirely pastoral and was not concerned with dogma. In fact, two of its constitutions were dogmatic, namely *Lumen Gentium*, the Council's key document, whose title is 'Dogmatic Constitution on the Church' and *Dei Verbum*, entitled 'Dogmatic Constitution on Divine Revelation'. There is indeed a second document with the Church as its subject, namely, 'Pastoral Constitution on the Church in the Modern World', otherwise known as *Gaudium et Spes*.

It is *Lumen Gentium* which speaks of the *sensus fidei*, 'the sense of faith'. It does so in a context where the Church is considered as reflecting in itself the triple office of Christ as priest, prophet and king.[20] Its observations on the sense of faith are made in connection with the People's participation in Christ's prophetic office and are as follows:

> The body of the faithful as a whole, anointed as they are by the Holy One (cf. 1 John 2:20, 27), cannot err in matters of belief. Thanks to a supernatural sense of the faith which characterizes the People as a whole, it manifests this unerring quality when, 'from the bishops down to the last

member of the laity' it shows universal agreement in matters of faith and morals.

For, by this sense of faith which is aroused and sustained by the Spirit of truth, God's People accepts not the word of men but the very Word of God (cf. 1 Thess. 2:13). It clings without fail to the faith once delivered to the saints (cf. Jude 3), penetrates it more deeply by accurate insights, and applies it more thoroughly to life. All this it does under the lead of a sacred teaching authority to which it loyally defers.[21]

Chapter Five

The Laity

Notwithstanding the emphasis that we have found in Scripture, the Church Fathers and the Councils on the *sensus fidelium* as a gift to the Church as a whole, contemporary theological reflection, as has been seen, tends to be most concerned with the sense of the faithful as a charism of the laity. That being the case it is appropriate to consider the question: Who are the laity? Bishop Ullathorne once put this question to Newman. The bishops of his day held the view that the lay province was, first and foremost, 'to hunt, to shoot, to entertain'. Judging from that attitude, we fancy that Ullathorne would have asked the question rather as though he might well have added, 'that thou art mindful of them' or even, 'Do they really exist?' (Newman's reply to the Bishop was to the effect that the Church would look foolish without them.)[1] We saw something of Newman's concern for the laity in Jan Walgrave's address (in Chapter 2) and will see more when we come to consider Newman's association with the *Rambler* and his article *On Consulting the Faithful in Matters of Doctrine* (to be dealt with in the next chapter). In his desire for a better evaluation of lay people in the Church, Newman was not quite alone. Another from his own era who shared his feelings is to be found in Antonio Rosmini. In his study entitled *The Five Wounds of the Church*, first published in

1846, Rosmini saw the first wound as the division between people and clergy at worship. He also wished for a greater awareness of the laity's dignity as members of the Church. After the time of Rosmini and Newman, much was written about lay activity and the forms it should take but very little about the laity's theological significance. We are familiar now, since the Second Vatican Council, with the acknowledgement of their ecclesial standing. Prior to the Council, the first serious attempt at a full theological study of the laity's position in the Church was the work by Yves Congar published in English translation in 1957 under the title *Lay People in the Church* to which I have already made several references (in Chapters 1 and 4). Congar saw the study of the laity as inseparable from a rethinking of the entire theology of the Church. Ecclesiology, together with ecumenism, was for him a lifelong passion, as we learn from his fellow Dominican, Fr Aidan Nichols, to whom I am indebted for the ensuing biographical details.[2] I shall follow them with some facts concerning Fr Nichols' own life and work.

Congar: Life and Influences

Yves Congar, OP, was born on 13 May 1904 at Sedan in the French Ardennes. His childhood friends were Jewish and Protestant, a circumstance which would have been unusual at that time, and in which his vocation to ecumenism began. In 1921 he entered the Parisian seminary known as 'of the Carmelites'; thereafter, in 1925, he joined the Dominican study-house of Le Saulchoir, then at Kain-la-Tombe in Belgium, its earlier personnel having been refugees there from the anti-clerical legislation of the Third French Republic. The Dominican house provided teaching of the highest university standard. Fr Congar himself was to spend much of his life as a teacher there. He was ordained to the priesthood on 25 July 1930. At the outbreak of the Second World War he was mobilized as a military chaplain. He was for some time a prisoner of war at Colditz!

While he was a student at Le Saulchoir, Congar was influenced by the enthusiasm of his master, Marie-Dominique Chenu, for the Ecumenical Movement, then in its early stages. In his mature years he was to do much travelling in its cause, both in France and abroad. For example, he regularly preached the Christian Unity Octave in one or another of the cities of France; his foreign travels included visits to England where he acquired knowledge of the history of the Anglican tradition; he made a lecture tour during the winter of 1953–4 in the Near East as a result of which his ecumenical links came to be especially concentrated on the Orthodox.

Congar's writings on ecumenism and ecclesiology were viewed with suspicion by the authorities in Rome. Eventually he was forbidden to teach or to publish his research and was exiled for a time to the École Biblique in Jerusalem and, in November 1954, to Blackfriars in Cambridge. He returned to France in December 1955 when Bishop Weber of Strasbourg welcomed him into his diocese where he was able to resume a ministry as pastor and theologian. Following the calling by Pope John XXIII of a General Council, Congar was appointed a consultor to the preparatory commission (surprisingly, in view of Rome's previous strictures). At the Council itself, he worked on many of its major documents including *Lumen Gentium* (the 'Dogmatic Constitution on the Church') and

Dei Verbum (the 'Dogmatic Constitution on Divine Revelation'). Congar died in 1995 having been made a cardinal by Pope John Paul II the previous year. He is the author of numerous works on many theological themes some of which naturally reflect his special interest in ecumenism and ecclesiology.[3]

Fr Aidan Nichols

John Christopher Aidan Nichols, OP, was born at Lytham St Annes, Lancashire on 17 September 1948. A former Anglican, he was received into the Catholic Church in 1966. He was a student at Christ Church College, Oxford and obtained a First Class degree in Modern History. After entering the Dominican order he spent seven years at Blackfriars, Oxford and was ordained to the priesthood during that time. Thereafter he moved to Edinburgh where he served as a Catholic Chaplain and took his PhD degree. Between 1983 and 1991 he was Lecturer in Dogmatics and Ecumenics at the Pontifical University of St Thomas Aquinas (the Angelicum) in Rome. He was awarded a Licentiate in Theology from the Angelicum. From Rome he moved back to Cambridge where he became Assistant Catholic Chaplain and subsequently, in 1988, an Affiliated University Lecturer. He was Prior of St Michael's in Cambridge from 1998 to 2004 and still lives at the priory when in England. Fr Nichols is the author of many works on a wide range of theological subjects.[4]

Who are the Laity?

For a fuller answer to the question which, as we saw above, Bishop Ullathorne put to Newman, we turn again to Congar's *Lay People* where he supplies the derivation and meaning of the expression 'layman'.[5] The word comes from the Greek *Laikos*. This is ultimately derived from *Laos*, meaning 'People', and because *Laos* is used in opposition to the word *Ethne* with its meaning of 'the peoples' or 'the gentiles', being pagans, *Laos* means specifically 'the consecrated people', 'the People of God'. Insofar as *Laikos* is linked to *Laos* it means that the *laikos*, the layman, is a member of God's consecrated people, and shares in its royal, priestly and prophetic calling; but *Laikos* differs from *Laos* by being the specific term by which a member of the *Laos* is distinguished from the priest or Levite who is also a member of the *Laos*. Congar goes on to point out that there is no distinction between 'lay people' and 'clerics' in the vocabulary of the New Testament (albeit, one must add, that the reality of the sacrificing priesthood was always present). The first use of the word 'layman' as distinct from 'priest' was in Clement's letter to the Corinthians (40.5; c.90 AD). The term specifies 'simple', in the sense of not being specially qualified, members among God's people, the whole of whom, as we have noted, are consecrated. So 'lay' signifies an element among the holy people. Congar wrote prior to the Second Vatican Council, which describes the laity in similar terms:

> The term laity is here understood to mean all the faithful except those in holy orders and those in a religious state sanctioned by the Church. These faithful are by baptism made one body with Christ and are established among the

People of God. They are in their own way made sharers in the priestly, prophetic and kingly functions of Christ. They carry out their own part in the mission of the whole Christian people with respect to the Church and the world.[6]

The Subjects of the *Sensus Fidelium*

As was remarked earlier, in the discourse of contemporary theologians, the emphasis often seems to shift from the whole Church to the laity as the *fideles*, the possessors of the *sensus fidelium*. It must be said that *Lumen Gentium* and *Christifideles Laici*[7] could be seen to provide some justification for that emphasis on the laity, bringing as they do what has been generally felt to be a much needed acknowledgement and encouragement of (to use the title of the latter document) 'The Vocation and Mission of the Lay Faithful in the Church and the World'. But attention has to be paid to what these documents actually do say, not what they may be reputed to have said, repute often differing from actuality in this respect. *Lumen Gentium*, in its chapter on 'The Laity', affirms at the outset that all the Council has previously said on the subject of the People of God, which is to say the entire Christian body, applies equally to the laity (for example, the sharing in the kingly, priestly and prophetic offices of Christ). But the concern of this section of the document is to point out 'certain things which pertain in a particular way to the laity'. The laity, whose gifts and services must be recognized by their pastors are to cooperate with the pastors in the saving mission of the Church; this they do 'according to their proper roles'. A secular character is proper and special to laymen. The vocation of the laity is to seek the kingdom of God by engaging in temporal affairs and by ordering them according to the plan of God.[8] *Christifideles Laici* enlarges on the meaning of the term 'secular' as used by *Lumen Gentium*, insisting that it be understood not only in a sociological but most especially in a theological sense. The Church herself, according to Pope Paul VI, 'has an authentic secular dimension, inherent in her inner nature and mission, which is deeply rooted in the mystery of the Word Incarnate, and which is realized in different forms through her members'. The world itself is destined to glorify God the Father in Christ; that is why the world comes to be a proper place for the fulfilment of a Christian vocation. As partakers in Christ's kingly office, the lay faithful are called to restore creation to its original value. God has handed over the world to men and women so that they may participate in the work of creation, free creation from the influence of sin and sanctify themselves in whatever their state and circumstances.[9] Among the modern theologians whose views have been mentioned above, there is a tendency to deduce from the secular character of the laity, not so much a secular as a theological mission. Their situation in the world is seen as making them a *locus theologicus*, not as attesting to apostolic dogma but opposing it.

It might be thought that the *sensus fidelium*, belonging as it does to the whole Church, from the bishops to the latest lay catechumen, cannot exist or validly operate independently in one particular body in the Church, for example the laity. (This point was touched upon in connection with the gift of the *sensus fidelium* to the individual believer.) Yet *Lumen Gentium* and *Christifideles Laici* do not seem to allow the conclusion to be drawn that the sense of the faith belongs only to the whole body of believers together. *Christifideles*, with citations from *Lumen Gentium*, declares:

> United to Christ, 'the great prophet' (Luke 7:16), and in the Spirit made 'witnesses' of the Risen Christ, the lay faithful are made sharers in the appreciation of the Church's supernatural faith, that 'cannot err in matters of belief' and sharers as well in the grace of the word (cf. Acts 2:17–18; Rev. 19:10).[10]

Nevertheless, there are to be found in post-conciliar theology, as we have seen, claims on behalf of the laity's 'appreciation', made, expressly or otherwise, in the name of the Council, which deserve to be questioned.

Such claims, in some of the essays we have studied, were on these lines. The laity, especially in moral questions, have an involvement in the world such that they can bring from the world to the Church a more practical and more authentic appreciation of moral imperatives than would otherwise be found; the magisterium would do well in certain instances to adapt its formulations in accordance with this kind of lay perception. Against such an argument it is suggested here that the key to a correct evaluation of the status of the lay understanding vis-à-vis that of the magisterium is the word 'sharers' used in *Christifideles Laici* as quoted above. The laity's endowment with the *sensus fidei* (the 'sense of the faith', the expression used in *Lumen Gentium*) is well assured, then. That does not mean we can allow that the *sensus fidei* of the laity can legitimately take a different path from that taken by the magisterium on faith and morals. As we shall see from Congar, the body of the faithful is only infallible when it listens to the teaching Church. The laity share this faculty as members of the entire People of God; the laity have the sense of the faith *qua* laity but it is not enjoyed otherwise than in common and in communion with the Pope and the magisterium.

The superior showing of the laity during the Arian crisis, famously attested to by Newman and, it should be noted from his account, made in common with their 'parish priests' and many of the monks, was not a case of the people being in opposition to the bishops. It was a case of the people being faithful to their baptism (which carries with it the prophetic gift) whereas the hierarchy were not always true to their office. The laity did not oppose apostolic teaching; they bore better witness to it than the body of the bishops. Newman would sympathize with the dislike, often shown by our present-day theologians, of any attempt to accord to the laity a mere passive role in any ecclesial sphere proper to them; yet for him the *sensus fidelium* at work in the laity could be relied upon to mirror and attest to apostolic teaching. Neither Newman, the Second Vatican Council nor *Christifideles* depicts the body of the laity as having some special perception of what is morally permissible to the Christian peculiar to itself, a perception which can be more in accordance with true Christian inspiration than that of the hierarchy, for instance. As our examples above have shown, some post-conciliar theologians do come close to making such a claim. Congar approvingly cites a colleague's remark that it is better to speak of 'sense of faith' than 'sense of the faithful'. This observation is shown to be much to the point, in view of the theology of the *sensus fidelium* that we saw in the post-conciliar authors. The use of 'sense of faith' would avoid giving the faithful at large a monopoly at the expense of theologians and of the pope and bishops.[11] One must qualify this, however, in view of the alliance of theologians and the 'pragmatic' laity which we saw in those authors and which was much to the fore when *Humanae Vitae* first appeared.

Congar on the *Sensus Fidelium*

We have heard the views of those theologians whose interpretation of the Second Vatican Council were considered, followed by a study of Newman's theology in relation to that of the post-conciliar writers and a history of the *sensus fidelium* derived from the Scriptures and the Church Councils (Chapters 2 to 4). I will now pay special attention to Yves Congar's thought. With his 1953 work, *Lay People in the Church*, he was, as remarked above, a pioneer in the theological study of the laity's ecclesial position; moreover, he came to have a strong influence on Vatican II's deliberations on the subject.

Congar's consideration of the *sensus fidelium* is linked to the exercise of papal infallibility. He stresses that this infallibility comes about not by means of a revelation but of a help; by virtue of this help the pope is kept from error when, as supreme teacher and shepherd, he pronounces definitively on a matter of faith or morals. The help is given to him in order that he may define the faith of the Church, which he must 'investigate and ascertain by appropriate means'; until it is so ascertained, it exists in the Church in a more or less obscure manner. It is in that connection that Congar introduces his account. He tells us that *sensus* or *consensus fidelium* is one of a set of terms with similar but not exactly the same meaning belonging as they do to different moments in history and different points of view. The other terms he mentions are *sensus Ecclesiae, sensus catholicus, sensus fidei*, adding *Christiani populis fides* and *communis Ecclesiae fides* as terms used with regard to the consultations preceding the pronunciation of the dogma of the Assumption. (Congar observes how the extraordinary development of Marian doctrine has been carried on by the people's faith and devotion, with the encouragement of their bishops, sometimes even in the teeth of the opinions of theologians.) The various designations of this *sensus* in the Church rest on a common basis of which Congar presents the following formulation:

> [T]here is a gift of God (of the Holy Spirit) which relates to the twofold reality, objective and subjective, of faith (*fides quae creditur; fides qua creditur*) which is given to the hierarchy and the whole body of faithful together ... and which ensures an indefectible faith to the Church.[12]

There are four aspects of the gift to be noted from Congar's exposition. First, this gift pertains both to the objective reality, the deposit of faith (*fides quae creditur*), and the subjective reality, the grace of faith in the believer (*fides qua creditur*). Secondly, the 'sense' is the gift of the Holy Spirit. Thus we can add here that any claim made for a view that it belongs to the *sensus fidelium* must be measured against what we know of the ways of the Spirit. Thirdly, Congar shows, as does *Lumen Gentium*, that the gift is not to one category of persons within the Church as distinct from others in such a way that one category could be at loggerheads with another, for instance, say, to the laity, or to all non-hierarchical members, as opposed to the hierarchy. It is made to the hierarchy and the whole body of faithful together. Fourthly, the gift of indefectibility ensures that until the end of time the Church will preserve her fidelity to the truth of the Gospel.

We saw how Congar began his analysis with a reference to papal infallibility which led him to that universal traditional infallibility which is the faith of the entire Church.

Infallibility

In discussions about the *sensus fidelium*, one sometimes meets with the expression 'the infallibility of the laity' and finds it not infrequently coupled with the name of Newman. The appropriateness of the use of the word at all as applied to the laity is doubtful. It could wrongly carry the suggestion that the laity have an independent infallibility peculiar to themselves and is not endorsed by Newman, as will be seen when we come to study his work *On Consulting the Faithful*. Certainly, as Newman and others have shown, the faith of the generality of believers has been appealed to in the Church's history, but appealed to as a sure expression of her dogmatic tradition. We saw (in Chapter 3) how Aidan Nichols explains the basis for such appeals, that is: 'Since all Christians are illuminated by Christ the internal teacher, they are enabled not just to receive the truth but "to make approval of that doctrine, to receive that doctrine as the truth".' He further comments:

> Just as the magisterium of the Church cannot err in what it teaches, so the laity, the consensus of the faithful, cannot be deceived in what they believe. The gift of teaching Christian truth without deceiving is a useless gift unless it is matched by some sort of reciprocal gift of believing, some gift of infallibly receiving infallible teaching among the laity.[13]

There is a problem with the word 'infallible' because there is a widespread misunderstanding of its meaning, not least among the laity. Often the meaning of the word is taken to be such that its opposite in meaning is 'fallible' or 'liable to be wrong'. The result is that if, say, in the case of a papal pronouncement on faith or morals, there is reason to think that its circumstances do not meet *ex cathedra* requirements, then the assent of the faithful may be withheld on the grounds that the pronouncement has not the status of dogma and so is not indisputably true. That argument overlooks the infallibility of the whole Church whose traditional doctrine on a particular matter will have preceded, possibly by centuries, the eventual papal definition, as was the case with *Humanae Vitae*. In any event the teaching of *Lumen Gentium* has to be kept in mind, namely that 'religious submission of will and of mind must be shown in a special way to the authentic teaching authority of the Roman Pontiff, even when he is not speaking *ex cathedra*.'[14]

Where two or three lay people are gathered together disputing the Church's teaching, 'We are the Church' is a claim sometimes heard. The state of the laity's belief may well represent the *fides Ecclesiae* as happened on the occasion of the definition of the Immaculate Conception, but can we therefore correctly say that the laity were infallible in the matter as though their infallibility were peculiar to their condition? According to Congar, all infallibility in the Church must be expressly referred to the working of the Holy Spirit. When that is done it can be seen that

> ... each is acted on in view of an infallibility, (finally one) according to his place in the body, receiving the infallibility that belongs to him in function of the infallibility of the total

organism ... The loving and believing Church is infallible only when it listens to the teaching Church and thus partakes of *the teaching Church's* infallibility.[15]

Thus, Congar shows us that it would be entirely wrong to look on the laity as either being able to play a trump card which makes the whole exercise of inerrancy in a magisterial decision as ultimately claimable by them, or else as having a right of veto over it. Not that Congar would subscribe to a view of the faithful as having only such infallibility as derives from a mere passive attention to the hierarchy. Nor, on the other hand, would he say that the role of the hierarchy is ever limited to a mere sanctioning of the opinions of the faithful. Both these mistaken views overlook the working of the Holy Spirit. The faithful's infallibility is not in mere deference to the hierarchy 'but it is of a vital, moral, nature connected with righteous living'. This reference to the faithful's way of life calls to mind a similar reference in *Lumen Gentium* §12, where it speaks of God's People as applying the faith more thoroughly to life as their insight deepens.

Finally, in view of the opposition to *Humanae Vitae* which came about since he wrote, it is appropriate to recall this observation from Congar:

> If it be right that the *sensus fidelium* or *sensus catholicus* is a power of adhesion and discernment in the body of the faithful, it is also and conjointly a sense of oneness and fellowship in which an essential element is an obedient attitude towards apostolical authority living in the episcopal body. Such is St Ignatius Loyola's rule, '*Bene sentire in Ecclesia.*'[16]

That such an attitude is an essential constituent of the *sensus fidelium* has not been to the fore so far in the theology of the subject. Nor were oneness and fellowship much exhibited in the Church as a result of the promulgation of the 1968 encyclical of Paul VI. Thus, there seems to be little strength in the argument that its rejection came about from any 'sense of the Church'.

Chapter Six

On Consulting the Faithful in Matters of Doctrine

The *Rambler* Controversy

Newman's teaching on the *sensus fidelium* is contained in his essay *On Consulting the Faithful in Matters of Doctrine* which appeared in the July 1859 issue of the *Rambler*, a journal which had been carried on by laymen prior to Newman's appointment as editor in that year.[1] The *Rambler* had the aim of presenting a Catholic interpretation of questions of the day and raising intellectual standards among English Catholics. Its quality was equal to that of the great periodicals of the time, for instance, the *Quarterly Review*. It enjoyed a high reputation and exerted a considerable influence among both Catholics and non-Catholics. At the time when Newman became involved, it had incurred the disapproval of the English Catholic bishops because of its daring theology and critical attitude towards ecclesiastical authority; not least in question was the acerbic tone of one of its co-editors, an Oxford convert clergyman, Richard Simpson.

The immediate chain of events which was to culminate in Newman's *On Consulting the Faithful* had begun with the appearance in the 1859 January and February issues of the *Rambler* of two articles by Scott Nasmyth Stokes, a

Catholic schools inspector and the leading Catholic lay
authority on educational matters, in which he urged that
Catholics should cooperate with the Newcastle
Commission. The Commission had been appointed in 1858
to report on ways of extending 'cheap and sound
elementary instruction to all classes of the people'. One of
the problems was how to reconcile the freedom of
denominational schools with public control over the
subsidies they received.[2] Unknown to the author and
editor, the bishops had already, in the preceding
November, made a decision concerning their attitude to the
Commission, their decision being not to cooperate, but did
not make it known until the spring, by which time, of
course, the articles had appeared. The bishops' judgement
was published in the May *Rambler*, the first issue under
Newman's editorship.

Newman's appointment as editor had come about as the
result of a meeting of several of the bishops held in London
when it was decided that unless Richard Simpson retired
from the editorship and the spirit of the journal changed,
they would be obliged to pass censure on it in their
forthcoming pastoral letters. They were reluctant to do so
as such a course would have meant a public scandal, and
the disowning of a journal which was influential and
respected both in the Catholic community and beyond it.
They approached Newman, who was *persona grata* with
both the bishops and the offending laity, begging him to
procure the resignation of Simpson. This would leave them
with the problem of finding a new editor acceptable to both
themselves and the proprietors of the *Rambler*. Another
layman closely concerned with the magazine, and one of
its owners, Sir John Acton, was equally unacceptable to
the bishops. It became clear that the only person who

would have the trust of both parties was Newman. He became editor in March 1859 at the urgent request of his own bishop, Ullathorne, and Cardinal Wiseman. He accepted against his own inclination and only after much prayer and deliberation, looking on the undertaking as the greatest 'mortification' of his life.[3] Having retired from the rectorship of the Catholic University of Ireland the previous year, he had been hoping for a rest before returning to his former studies, after which he hoped to begin a substantial work of theology.[4] But his conscience obliged him to do his utmost to keep the *Rambler* in print. His purpose in accepting the editorship was to serve the educated laity and to keep afoot an organ which he believed exercised a vital apostolate. In addition, he wished to assist the efforts of the bishops to keep peace among Catholics. There were divisions among them arising in part from the existence of a body of converts who inclined towards faction, as some saw it, and a body of old Catholics. The converts tended to be suspected of not really possessing the Catholic spirit. Part of the trouble lay with the English bishops themselves. Most of them, having been educated abroad, had no real understanding of England and the English. It was Newman's policy, destined to be thwarted, to make the *Rambler* uncontroversial in tone and subject matter.

The first number under Newman's editorship came out in May 1859. The bishops' judgement on the Schools Commission question was published in this issue and Newman apologized for the Stokes articles, explaining that 'we did not know that the bishops had spoken formally'. He went on to say:

Acknowledging then, most fully the prerogatives of the episcopate, we do unfeignedly believe ... that their

Lordships really desire to know the opinion of the laity on subjects in which the laity are especially concerned. If even in the preparation of a dogmatic definition the faithful are consulted as lately in the instance of the Immaculate Conception, it is at least as natural to anticipate such an act of kind feeling and sympathy in great practical questions.

A furore was to ensue upon his reference to the consultation of the faithful.

In this same editorial, Newman continued with much earnestness to express regret for any seeming disrespect in the words or tone of the articles even though the supposition behind them, namely, that the bishops would like to know the feelings of an influential portion of the laity before taking any irrevocable steps, could surely not itself be disrespectful. Anything tending towards the misery of division between the rulers of the Church and the educated laity was to be deplored, and no such thing had been intended. After fervent assurance of confidence in the qualities of the bishops (which included generosity) towards their flocks, he concluded:

Let them pardon, then, the incidental hastiness of manner of the rude Jack-tars of their vessel, as far as it occurred, in consideration of the zeal and energy with which they haul-to the ropes and man the yards.[5]

On 13 May Newman received a letter from John Gillow, a professor of theology at Ushaw, protesting against the passage quoted above in which Newman referred to the consulting of the faithful by the bishops. On being asked to state the grounds of his objection Gillow wrote to explain that Newman's words seemed to mean that the infallibility of the Church resided in the laity rather than in the hierarchy. Newman replied that Gillow had misunderstood the word 'consult' and had taken it to mean asking for advice or an opinion. The word had been used in the sense that it is used of, for example, a barometer which 'does not give us its opinion but ascertains for us a fact'. Writing for readers among whom were laymen not versed in theology, he had not been using the word in the theological sense that Gillow had attached to it, which was 'to consult with'. Newman pointed out that Gillow was confusing the infallibility of the Church with the power and prerogative of definition, which latter did indeed belong exclusively to the hierarchy. As for infallibility, '. . . it resides *per modum unius* in both, as a figure is contained both on the seal and on the wax, and primarily in the mind of the engraver'.[6]

Bishop Ullathorne called on Newman on 22 May. He told him that even the May number of the *Rambler* (that is, the one edited by Newman) was too disturbing for Catholic taste. 'There were remains of the old spirit. It was irritating. Our laity were a *peaceable* set; the Church was *peace*. They had a deep faith; they did not like to hear that anyone doubted.' Newman countered this by saying that Ullathorne 'did not see the state of the laity', in Ireland, for example, where Newman knew from experience that they were unsettled, though docile. Newman's account goes on: 'He said something like "Who are the laity?" I answered (not these words) that the Church would look foolish without them.' He strove in vain to convince Ullathorne that he saw his, Newman's, work with the *Rambler* as having the same object as had taken him to Ireland, by which he meant his work in connection with the foundation of the Catholic University in Dublin during the preceding years of the 1850s.[7] This object was that which dominated all Newman undertook, namely, the intellectual and religious education of the Catholic laity aimed chiefly at cultivating the faculty of right and sound judgement. Christianity would be its governing spirit and would assimilate and give a character to literature and science. He desired the formation of a Catholic laity that could participate in the discussion of such ecclesiastical matters as pertained to those areas where their position and duties in society gave them a special experience and competence. In short, his wishes were such that they were destined to be taken up by the recommendation of §5 (on the laity) of the Second Vatican Council's *Lumen Gentium*. 'He would not allow the weight of anything I said,' Newman goes on to complain of Ullathorne. When he reminded the bishop of how unwilling he had been to take on the editorship in the first place, Ullathorne turned to him abruptly and said: 'Why not give it up?' Newman agreed instantly. Commenting on this readiness, he wrote: 'I never have resisted, nor can resist, the voice of a lawful superior speaking in his own province.'[8] The upshot of the meeting was agreement that he should give up the editorship after the next number which would be the July.

This record of the conversation between Newman and Ullathorne will have shown how obtuse and mentally hidebound were the bishops at that time and how ready to put a dead hand on any attempt at expansion of thought or aspiration. It is necessary to have some idea of their mentality, and of what little store they set by the laity, in order to see how Newman's *On Consulting the Faithful* could have had the disastrous consequences which it had. (Disastrous, that is to say, in the short term and for Newman himself; for his idea of the laity was to be taken up a hundred years later in full measure by the Second Vatican Council, whether with Newman's aims expressly in mind or not.) After the *Rambler* episode he lived under a cloud of suspicion and distrust. This caused him to cease writing during the years from 1859, the year of the *Rambler*, until 1864; previously he had written a book each year. His position of leadership in the Catholic sphere and his prestige among both Catholics and Anglicans was restored by his *Apologia* (1864). Even after that, suspicion and hostility towards him persisted in the officials and the leaders of the Church right up to the eve of his appointment as Cardinal, which took place in 1879 and which Manning and others had tried to prevent. A few years after the event, Pope Leo XIII remarked to an English visitor, 'My Cardinal! It was not easy, it was not easy. They said he was too liberal, but I had determined to honour the Church in honouring Newman.'[9]

On Consulting the Faithful in Matters of Doctrine is Newman's explanation of the sentence in his *Rambler* editorial which had provoked so much criticism. The 1961 edition of *On Consulting*, to which my references are made, was its first re-publication since Newman's time. The editor, John Coulson, points out the significance of the essay. He has this to say:

> The importance of *On Consulting the Faithful* is that it removes the argument from the realm of policy and discipline, and places it firmly in the context of theology; it has ceased to be a series of charges and counter-charges, a dispute about the Bishops' behaviour over a particular question of educational co-operation, and has become an argument about the laity's place in the very heart, mind and structure of the Church.[10]

Newman's *On Consulting the Faithful*

In this article Newman sets out to deal with two questions bearing upon doctrine which, it will be remembered, he had caused to be raised when, as the newly-appointed editor of the journal, he had written there an apology to the bishops for the Catholic school inspector's article urging cooperation with the educational Commission; the bishops unfortunately had made an as yet unannounced decision not to cooperate. Newman's offending statement was that: 'in the preparation of a dogmatic definition, the faithful are consulted . . .' The first question was whether it was doctrinally correct to say that an appeal to the sense of the faithful is one of the preliminaries of a doctrinal definition. The second was, granting that the faithful are taken into account, whether it is correct to say they are *consulted*. He deals first with the second question.

He begins with an explanation, on the same lines as that given in his correspondence with Gillow, of his use of the word 'consult'. He had not intended it to convey the technical meaning which a professional theologian, expressing himself in Latin, would give it, that is to say, to 'consult *with*' or to 'take *counsel*'. The readership of the *Rambler* included lay people who would not be doctrinally misled by the use of the word; as Newman remarks, 'English has innovated on the Latin sense of its own Latin words.' In its popular and ordinary use the word 'consult' includes the idea of inquiring into a matter of fact as well as asking for a judgement. We speak of consulting a watch or a sun-dial. 'A physician consults the pulse of his patient; but not in the same sense as his patient consults *him*.' At this point, while still explaining his use of the offending word 'consult', Newman begins to bring out the theological significance of this process of reference to the faithful when a dogmatic definition is to be made. He says:

> Doubtless their advice, their opinion, their judgment on the question of definition is not asked; but the matter of fact, viz. their belief, *is* sought for, as a testimony to that apostolical tradition, on which alone any doctrine whatsoever can be defined. In like manner, we may 'consult' the liturgies or the rites of the Church; ... [T]hey are witnesses to ... the doctrines which they contain ... And, in like manner, ... the *fidelium sensus* and *consensus* is a branch of evidence which it is natural or necessary for the Church to regard and consult, before she proceeds to any definition, from its intrinsic cogency; and by consequence, that it ever has been so regarded and consulted.[11]

After further discussion of semantics, he quotes a saying of St Dionysius, whose orthodoxy, like Newman's, had been impugned: 'But my accusers ... take up two little words detached from the context, and proceed to discharge them at me as pebbles from a sling.' Newman concludes this first section by asserting that theological accuracy of expression should not be looked for in popular works. If inexactness of expression is found, it should not immediately be attributed to self-will or undutifulness.[12]

Having left the question of wording, Newman goes on to assert the reality of appeal to the faithful prior to doctrinal pronouncements and the reason for it. The reason is 'because the body of the faithful is one of the witnesses to the fact of the tradition of revealed doctrine, and because their *consensus* through Christendom is the voice of the Infallible Church.' The tradition of the

Apostles manifests itself at various times throughout history and in various ways. Among the instances Newman gives are: through the hierarchy, sometimes by the people, or by scholars, by liturgy, and customs, 'by events, disputes, movements, and all those other phenomena which are comprised under the name of history.' None of these channels may be treated with disrespect; yet it must always be acknowledged 'that the gift of discerning, discriminating, defining, promulgating, and enforcing any portion of that tradition resides solely in the *Ecclesia docens*.'[13]

People vary, Newman remarks, as to which aspect of doctrine each has a tendency to emphasize. He says that he himself is accustomed to lay great stress on the *consensus fidelium*, then goes on to explain how that came about.

In his study of the Church Fathers he had found that he was unable to trace certain parts of the defined doctrine of the Church in ecclesiastical writers. His problem was that up to the date of the definition of certain articles of doctrine there was very deficient evidence from existing documents that Bishops, doctors and theologians held those doctrines. While he was in Rome in 1847 preparing for the Catholic priesthood, he had the opportunity of discussing the point with Perrone, the professor of dogma at the Collegio Romano, who spoke of the *sensus fidelium* as compensating for any deficiency in patristic testimony with regard to various points of dogma.[14]

The following year, Newman was able to read a newly published treatise by Perrone on the Immaculate Conception which included references to the *sensus fidelium* and its bearing upon the doctrine which was the subject of the work. Newman discusses this dogma, so far as it relates to the *sensus fidelium*, beginning with references to Perrone's treatise, and making five main points:

First, Perrone states the historical fact of the *sensus*. Speaking of the *Ecclesiae sensus* (the sense of the Church) on the subject of the Immaculate Conception, he says that, even though the liturgies of the Feast of the Conception made it sufficiently clear what the feeling of the Church was on the subject, it might be worth while for him to comment on the sense of the Church itself. He then says that it is gathered from a twofold source, that is, from the pastors, and from the faithful. The importance Newman attaches to this observation, in view of what is to follow in his argument, is that Perrone not only joins together the pastors and the faithful but contrasts them: 'I mean,' says Newman, '"the faithful" do not *include* the "pastors".'

Then Perrone goes on, Newman tells us, to describe the relationship of the *sensus fidelium* to the *sensus Ecclesiae*. Perrone says that to enquire into the sense of the Church on any question is simply to investigate to which side of it she has been more inclined. The signs ('*indicia*' – Perrone is writing in Latin) of what has been the Church's inclination consist of 'her public acts, liturgies, feasts, prayers, "pastorum ac *fidelium* in unum veluti conspiratio"' (the convergence of pastors and faithful in a particular respect). Again, Newman is making the point, when he places 'fidelium' in italics, that the faithful have their own witness, howbeit there is complete union between theirs and that of their pastors.

Perrone's third point is that these various *indicia* are also the 'instruments' of tradition and vary in the strength of the evidence they give in favour of particular doctrines. The strength of one makes up in a particular case for the deficiency of another. Thus, 'the strength of the "sensus communis fidelium" can make up (e.g.) for the silence of the Fathers.'

Fourthly, Perrone then speaks expressly of the force of the *sensus fidelium* as distinct (not separate, adds Newman) from the teaching of their pastors. He maintains that the most eminent theologians have been unanimous in attributing the status of proof to 'the universal sense of the faithful people' as regards the holding by the Church of an article of faith. Perrone quotes one of them as arguing that, when there is a dispute concerning the Christian faith, the feeling of 'Christian men formed in doctrine and faith' is to be enquired into. Newman remarks that these expressions, though not conveying the sense of the asking of advice, do imply a certain deference towards the persons addressed. Another saying, quoted by Perrone from St Gregory, goes: '[I]n definitions of the faith regard is to be had (*habenda ratio*) as far as possible, to the consensus of the faithful.' Newman points out that '*habere rationem*', to have regard to, 'is an act of respect and consideration.' However, as Gregory's discourse as cited by Perrone proceeds, it is found giving far more serious weight than that to the consent of the faithful. In Newman's words:

> Thus Gregory says that, in controversy about a matter of faith, the consent of all the faithful has such a force in the proof of this side or that, that the Supreme Pontiff is *able and ought* to *rest* upon it, as being *the judgement or sentiment* of the *infallible* Church. These are surely exceedingly strong words; not that I take them to mean strictly that infallibility is *in* the 'consensus fidelium', but

that that 'consensus' is an *indicium* or *instrumentum* to us of the judgement of that Church which *is* infallible.

This last sentence contains an important observation on Newman's part, and to be borne in mind when the expression 'the infallibility of the laity' is met with, whether coupled with the name of Newman or of the Second Vatican Council. If the expression is bandied about without close attention to the way it is qualified by those using it, it can convey the impression that, failing all others, including the hierarchy, the laity will, if allowed, come to the rescue of the truth.

Newman also draws attention to Perrone's use of the image of a seal in speaking of the *sensus fidelium*. After mentioning various arguments in favour of the Immaculate Conception, such as the testimony of universities, religious bodies and theologians, Perrone declares: 'At length the unanimity of the whole Christian people [*totius Christiani populi consensus*] stamps all these with as it were the firmest seal.'

Lastly, Perrone gives several instances in which the definition of a doctrine by the magisterium of the Church, notably the declaration that the saints enjoy the beatific vision even before the resurrection, was made solely in consequence of attention to the *sensus fidelium*.[15]

Having dealt with Perrone's treatise, Newman turns his attention to the papal Encyclical Letter which appeared prior to the definition of the dogma of the Immaculate Conception in which the Pope asked the Bishops of the Catholic world to inform him of the feeling of 'vester clerus *populusque fidelis*' (your clergy and your faithful people – he is still quoting Perrone) towards the doctrine and its definition. The ascertainment of the feeling of the faithful on this occasion was the very event which he had stated in his earlier *Rambler* commentary to have happened. 'It seems to me important to keep this in view, whatever becomes of the word "consulted", which, I have already said, is not to be taken in its ordinary Latin sense.'

In 1854 the definition of the Immaculate Conception took place, and the Papal Bull containing it appeared. In it the Pope referred to previous enquiries, saying that although he already knew the sentiments of the Bishops, he wished to know those of the people also. Newman remarks how, before it gives the formal definition, the Bull enumerates the various witnesses to the apostolicity of the doctrine, including tradition, the 'perpetual sense of the Church', and the 'conspiratio' of the Catholic Bishops and the faithful. '*Conspiratio* [repeats Newman]; the two, the Church teaching and the Church taught, are put together, as one twofold testimony, illustrating each other, and never to be divided.'

Newman concludes this section of his paper with comments on an extract from a treatise by Bishop Ullathorne on the Immaculate Conception, written a year or two after the papal definition. The Bishop remarks that 'the universal conviction of pious Catholics' is of no small account and should not be overlooked in a doctrinal argument; 'for that pious belief, and the devotion which springs from it, are the *faithful reflection* of the pastoral teaching.' Newman comments: 'Reflection; that is, the people are a *mirror*, in which the Bishops see themselves.' He then remarks wryly, doubtless with his ill-fated use in the *Rambler* of the word 'consult' in mind, 'Well, I suppose a person may *consult* his glass, and in that way may know things about himself which he can learn in no other way.'

Newman quotes further from Bishop Ullathorne:

> The more devout the faithful grew, the more devoted they showed themselves towards this mystery. And it is the devout who have the surest instinct in discerning the mysteries of which the Holy Spirit breathes the grace through the Church, and who, with as sure a tact, reject what is alien from her teaching. The common accord of the faithful has weight much as an argument even with the most learned divines.

At this point Ullathorne cites a number of observations made by St Augustine regarding this 'common accord of the faithful'. For example, 'It seems that I have believed nothing but the confirmed opinion and the exceedingly wide-spread report of populations and nations.'[16]

Newman here mentions his intention of dealing with an historical instance of this same great principle, an instance not mentioned by Ullathorne; he is referring to the witness of the faithful against Arianism.[17] This was to attract further hostile criticism, and suspicion of heresy.

But first he states the several ways in which, according to theologians, the consent of the faithful bears upon the manifestation of the tradition of the Church. He perceives five ways in which the *consensus* of the faithful is to be regarded. The first of these is as a testimony to the fact of the apostolic dogma. This point is sufficiently well illustrated, he says, in the foregoing passages from Fr Perrone. The feature of the *sensus fidelium* that Newman mentions secondly is 'a sort of instinct, or φρονημα (*phronēma*) deep in the bosom of the mystical body of Christ.' He explains this by referring to a passage in

Möhler's *Symbolique*. The action of the Holy Spirit in the Church, Möhler says, brings about in her members an instinct, an eminently Christian feeling for the truths of the faith. 'This common sentiment,' he continues, 'this conscience of the Church is tradition in the subjective sense of the word.' He then explains this 'subjective' tradition as 'the Christian sense existing in the Church, and transmitted by the Church; a sense, however, which cannot be separated from the truths which it holds, since it is formed from and by those truths.' This last comment of Möhler's recalls the insistence by several of our contemporary theologians that the *sensus fidelium* is intrinsic to faith.

A 'direction of the Holy Ghost' is the third of the qualities which Newman attributes to this Christian sense. He explains it by reference to the theologian Petavius, quoting Cardinal Fisher, in a passage where Fisher speaks of a custom imperceptibly gaining a position, 'not by any force of precept but by a certain tacit consent of both people and clergy' before being established by any conciliar decree. Fisher adds: 'This custom has its birth *in that people which is ruled by the Holy Ghost* ...' This third attribute would seem to touch on the very problem which Newman had encountered in his reading where he had sometimes been unable to trace any evidence from bishops and theologians of the holding of a doctrine prior to its official definition.

The fourth of the ways in which he regards the *sensus fidelium* is as an answer to the prayer of the Mystical Body. Petavius is again quoted, this time commending a saying of St Augustine, that sometimes God makes revelations to the minds of individuals, not only by extraordinary means such as visions, but also 'in those usual ways, according to which what is unknown to them is opened *in answer to their prayer*. After this manner it is to be believed that God has revealed to Christians the sinless Conception of the Immaculate Virgin.'

Newman explains the fifth characteristic of the *sensus fidelium*, which he describes as 'jealousy of error, which it immediately perceives as a scandal' by referring to the second of his own series of lectures called *Certain Difficulties felt by Anglicans in Catholic Teaching* from which he quotes:

> We know that it is the property of life to be impatient of any foreign substance in the body to which it belongs. It will be sovereign in its own domain, and it conflicts with what it cannot assimilate into itself, and is *irritated and disordered* till it has expelled it ... The religious life of a people is of a certain quality and direction, and these are tested by the mode in which it encounters the various opinions, customs, and institutions which are submitted to it ... [S]ubmit your heretical and Catholic principle to the action of the multitude, and you will be able to pronounce at once whether it is imbued with Catholic truth or with heretical falsehood.[18]

Bishops and People during the Arian Crisis

In order to illustrate his assertion that the way in which the voice of 'the multitude' can be relied on to bear truthful Christian testimony in the face of error, Newman takes up, in his *On Consulting the Faithful*, the example of the good part played by them during the Arian controversy of the fourth century which he had used for the same purpose in the lecture referred to above. He declares:

> It is not a little remarkable, that, though, historically speaking, the fourth century is the age of doctors, illustrated,

as it was, by the saints Athanasius, Hilary, the two Gregories, Basil, Chrysostom, Ambrose, Jerome, and Augustine, and all of these saints bishops also, except one, nevertheless in that very day the divine tradition committed to the infallible Church was proclaimed and maintained far more by the faithful than by the Episcopate.

As if he fears that this will prove a startling statement, he explains it as follows: He is not denying that the majority of bishops were personally orthodox; that there were members of the clergy who stood by and guided the laity; that it was from the bishops that the laity received their faith in the first instance; that ignorance, even active infidelity, did exist among the laity. Nevertheless:

> [I]n that time of immense confusion the divine dogma of our Lord's divinity was proclaimed, enforced, maintained, and (humanly speaking) preserved, far more by the 'Ecclesia docta' than by the 'Ecclesia docens'; that the body of the episcopate was unfaithful to its commission, while the body of the laity was faithful to its baptism.

At one time it was the Pope, Newman continues, at other times the great sees of the period, at other times general councils, which 'said what they should not have said, or did what obscured and compromised revealed truth; while, on the other hand, it was the Christian people who, under Providence, were the ecclesiastical strength of Athanasius, Hilary . . . and other great solitary confessors who would have failed without them.'

Newman sees in the history of Arianism a pre-eminent example of a state of the Church such that, in order to learn the tradition of the Apostles, we must have recourse to the faithful. He cites the factors, four in number, which make the Arian instance so very cogent: first, it occurs so early in the history of the teaching Church; secondly, the doctrine in question, the divinity of Christ, was fundamental to the faith; thirdly, the controversy and the disorder it caused were so long-lasting, that is to say almost sixty years; fourthly, the matter involved persecution, in life, limb, and property, to the faithful 'whose loyal perseverance decided it.' Newman then reiterates his contention that the Nicene dogma was maintained during the fourth century, not by the Holy See, Councils or Bishops, but by the *consensus fidelium*. On the subject of the failure of the Church authorities, he goes on to make this assertion:

> [T]hat there was a temporary suspense of the function of the 'Ecclesia docens.' The body of Bishops failed in their confession of the faith. They spoke variously one against another; there was nothing, after Nicaea, of firm, unvarying, consistent testimony, for nearly sixty years.[19]

There is a special quality which Newman sees in the testimony of the general faithful and to which he draws attention later in his article; this is that, being untaught in theology, they bring out and avow just what they believe in a straightforward, genuine manner. In this way they repeat the objective truth, whereas theologians and Church Fathers colour it 'with their own mental peculiarities.'[20]

Newman prefaces his account of the confusion after Nicaea with a brief reference to that Council and its decision. He notes that it took place in the year AD 325 and consisted of 318 bishops chiefly from the eastern provinces of Christendom, its purpose being to settle the question of Arianism (a heresy that failed to accept the full mystery of the two natures of Jesus Christ who is true

God and true man). The council anathematized Arianism
and inserted into the creed the clause which affirms that
the Son is 'consubstantial with the Father', thereby
establishing the dogma which Arianism impugned. He
adds that in the year AD 326 St Athanasius, the great
champion of the 'consubstantial' dogma, was elected
Bishop of Alexandria. He then proceeds to give abundant
examples from many parts of Christendom of the
'immense confusion' he has referred to and the failure of
steady witness to the Church's dogma by councils,
bishops and popes.

Among his examples are the synods of Caesarea and
Tyre held in AD 334 and 335 against Athanasius himself
which accused and condemned him for numerous heinous
crimes, deposed him from his see, forbade him for life to
set foot in Alexandria and banished him to Gaul. They
received Arius into communion. The Council of Rome,
AD 341, pronounced Athanasius innocent. Also in AD
341, the Great Council of the Dedication at Antioch
ratified the proceedings at Caesarea and Tyre, placed an
Arian in the see of Athanasius and decreed the reversal of
the 'consubstantial' formula. Four or five creeds, in place
of the Nicene, were successively adopted.[21]

Newman quotes the remarks of three of the saints of the
period. From St Jerome: 'Nearly all the churches in
the whole world, under the pretence of peace and the
emperor, are polluted with the communion of the Arians.'
He adds Jerome's famous dictum: 'Ingemuit totus orbis
terrarum et se esse Arianum miratus est.' ('The whole
world groaned and indeed was astonished to find itself
Arian.') Newman comments on Jerome's remark in a way
which seems to indicate that it was ironical. He relates it
to the Council of Ariminum (AD 359) where the bishops

who attended were so worn out by delaying tactics on the part of the Arians that they abandoned the 'consubstantial' formula of Nicaea and subscribed to the heretical formula substituted for it by the heretics. Newman interprets Jerome's words as meaning that the Catholics of Christendom were surprised indeed to find that the Council of Ariminum had made Arians of them.[22] From St Hilary Newman quotes: 'It is most dangerous to us, and it is lamentable, that there are at present as many creeds as there are sentiments, and as many doctrines among us as dispositions, while we write creeds and explain them according to our fancy.'[23] And from St Gregory: 'If I must speak the truth, I feel disposed to shun every conference of Bishops; for never saw I synod brought to a happy issue, and remedying, and not rather aggravating, existing evils.'[24]

Having illustrated from various authorities the shortcomings of the councils and bishops during the Arian years, Newman then endorses in a similar way his contention that it was by the 'consensus fidelium' that the Nicene dogma was maintained. Among the instances he gives, the first is of outrages in Alexandria, related by Athanasius, where, at the instigation of the Arian bishops, 'a multitude of herdsmen and shepherds, and dissolute youths belonging to the town, armed with swords and clubs' carried out brutal assaults on the people; their purpose was an attempt to force the people to join the Arians and receive the Arian bishop who had been sent to them by the Emperor and whom they had refused. A further example from Alexandria of the laity's courageous resistance to Arianism was given when orthodox worshippers were cruelly assaulted by a company of soldiers under their commander.[25]

Another instance of staunch popular witness cited by Newman took place in Edessa. There was a magnificent church in that city, dedicated to St Thomas the Apostle, where religious assemblies were continually held. The prefect incurred the displeasure of the visiting Emperor Valens when the Emperor learned that the prefect had failed to expel the usual congregation who were all opposed to Arianism. The prefect, in order to prevent wholesale slaughter, secretly warned them against resorting to the church since all who were found there would be put to death. In spite of this, the following day found them all either at the church or hurrying towards it, eager for martyrdom. The prefect reported to the Emperor that all were ready to die for their faith; he added that it would be preposterous to destroy so many people at one time, 'and thus succeeded in restraining the Emperor's wrath.'[26]

Another of Newman's examples describes the scene in Cappadocia where, according to St Basil, writing about the year 372, blasphemy and impiety were so rife that those of the laity who were sound in faith avoided the places of worship 'as schools of impiety' and prayed with anguished tears in solitude. Writing four years later, Basil tells how the people left the houses of prayer and assembled in desert places where they lived wretchedly in the open air exposed to extremes of bitter weather in the winter and in the summer to the scorching sun.[27]

Newman includes in his account of the fidelity of the laity references to the influence of the monks. St Anthony, for example, left the desert in order to go about Alexandria warning its inhabitants against Arianism and affirming that Athanasius alone preached the doctrines of the Apostles. The monks of Syria, Cappadocia and the neighbouring provinces were attached to the Nicene faith. Arians met with popular odium and aversion when the attitude of the monks towards their creed was observed.[28]

Constant Need for the *Sensus Fidelium*

Newman makes it clear that he is not supposing that such times as the Arian will ever come again. He sees the episcopate of his own age as evincing such fidelity to the Holy See and being so little disposed to innovation that 'if there ever was an age which might dispense with the testimony of the faithful, and leave the maintenance of the truth to the pastors of the Church, it is the age in which we live.' (Naturally, this was not a suitable occasion for him to give vent to his opinion that 'the age in which we live' was one of over-zealous opposition by those in authority to the least originality.) He suggests that this conservatism may be the reason why the 'consensus fidelium' has, in the minds of many, 'fallen into the background' at the time he is writing. But he goes on to add:

> Yet each constituent portion of the Church has its proper functions, and no portion can be safely neglected. Though the laity be but the reflection or echo of the clergy in matters of faith, yet there is something in the 'pastorum et fidelium *conspiratio*', [the agreement of pastors and faithful] which is not in the pastors alone.

This was illustrated, as Newman has shown, by the history of the definition of the Immaculate Conception when Pope Blessed Pius IX had been our exemplar 'of the duty of considering the sentiments of the laity upon a point of tradition, in spite of whatever fullness of evidence the Bishops had already thrown upon it.' The testimony of the faithful is always relevant, he maintains, when a magisterial definition is contemplated, but most especially when the doctrine bears directly on devotional sentiments. The Immaculate Conception, Newman's remarks on which in the *Rambler* he is now defending, is an instance, he says (evidently because it involves popular devotion to the Mother of God). Another is the very subject of his essay, the Arian heresy, where the divinity of Jesus Christ was impugned. The doctrine of the Real Presence and the cult of the saints are instances of the victorious witness of the faithful when there was perplexity or disagreement in the *ecclesia docens*.[29]

The Faithful and the Council of Ephesus

Newman concludes by quoting a stirring account by a contemporary and fellow Oratorian, J. D. Dalgairns, of the scenes at Ephesus in the year 431 when the Third General Council of the Church was held there. His account illustrates that 'While devotion in the shape of a dogma issues from the high places of the Church, in the shape of devotion ... it starts from below...' The Council had been summoned in an attempt to solve the mystery of how Jesus Christ could at one and the same time be truly God and truly man (as had been established at Nicaea). Nestorius and his adherents had been asserting that He must be two quite distinct persons, the divine Son of God and the merely human son of Mary. Thus, the deliberations bore upon the correctness or otherwise of calling Mary, the mother of Jesus, the Mother of God.

Dalgairns describes the anxiety of the people of Ephesus as they await the Council's decision; he shows

how they all, even the humblest, understand what point of
doctrine is at issue and how the keenness of their anxiety
is made keener still by the knowledge that many
influential personages, including Nestorius, Patriarch of
Constantinople, who has won the emperor's court over to
his side, together with at least eighty-four bishops of the
same mind as they, 'are coming to make out that their
own mother is not the Mother of God'; and, to add to the
suspense, there will be present the fence-sitting Bishop
John of the great see of Antioch.

The weariness and anxiety of the waiting populace
grew as the day wore on without a decision. But, at last,
'what a cry of joy bursts from the assembled crowd, as it
is announced to them that Mary has been proclaimed to
be, what every one with a Catholic heart knew that she
was before, the Mother of God!' Dalgairns then relates
how the crowd surrounded the Bishops with acclama-
tions; how they accompanied them to their lodgings with
a long torch-lit procession and burned incense before
them. 'There was but little sleep in Ephesus that night;
for very joy they remained awake.'

Finally, Newman has the following comment to make
on this description of the emotions and the concern of the
laity at Ephesus:

> I think certainly that the *Ecclesia docens* is more happy
> when she has such enthusiastic partisans about her ... than
> when she cuts off the faithful from the study of her divine
> doctrines ... and requires from them a *fides implicita* in her
> word, which in the educated classes will terminate in
> indifference, and in the poorer in superstition.[30]

Delation to Rome

During the July which saw the publication of *On Consulting*, Newman received a visit from Manning who was attending a synod at Oscott and had been sent to take him to task about the article. Bishop Brown of Newport had raised the subject with Wiseman, Ullathorne and Manning, and all agreed that Newman had used very unfortunate expressions when describing the short-comings of the teaching Church at the time of the Arian heresy. Newman assured Manning that he had not intended to say that the Church herself had fallen into error. The following month, Newman heard again from a troubled Dr Gillow. Gillow disputed that there could ever be, as Newman had said occurred during the fourth century, 'a temporary suspense of the functions of the Ecclesia docens', or that 'the body of Bishops could fail in their confession of the faith.'[31] To say that such a failure could occur in the Bishops seemed to Gillow to imply that, contrary to what he had always believed, the infallibility of the Church was not such that it resided in each and every part. He also challenged Newman's aspersions, as they seemed to him, on the Church's requirement of a *fides implicita* in her word. Newman replied that the word 'suspense' did not mean 'failure', that it has a far lighter meaning even that 'suspension'. By the 'body of the Bishops' he had not meant the *Ecclesia docens* but 'the actual mass at the particular time spoken of.' He does not deny that belief in the Holy Catholic Church involves *fides implicita* in her teaching; he was merely speaking of the possibility of inculcating in the faithful a sort of *fides implicita* which would terminate in the evils he mentioned.[32]

Without Newman's knowledge, the 'Consulting the Faithful' article was delated to Rome by Bishop Brown of Newport later in the same year. At the beginning of 1860 Bishop Ullathorne informed him of the delation, whereupon Newman instantly offered to explain all he had written, showing how it was in accordance with Catholic teaching. Cardinal Wiseman, who was to act as intermediary, was given by the Congregation of Propaganda a list of questions about the article for Newman to answer. Wiseman never gave this list to Newman; instead he sent him a message through Manning that he, Wiseman, would bring the matter to a satisfactory conclusion. In Rome, it was apparently concluded by those concerned that Newman had refused to comply. They remained for years under that misapprehension. The matter was apparently settled by means of a visit made to Rome by two Oratorian Fathers, St John and Bittleston, but neither there nor at home did Newman's reputation ever entirely recover from the affair.

Newman Answers His Critics

The accusations against 'On Consulting the Faithful' had been put into theological form by Franzelin, a Jesuit theologian, in a lecture at the Roman College. In an appendix to the third edition of his work, *The Arians of the Fourth Century*, in 1871,[33] Newman refuted Franzelin's objections, which had related to three of the former's assertions (though without naming Franzelin or expressly referring to his lecture). On the visit to Rome of Fathers St John and Bittleston, it had been agreed on the advice of Perrone that Newman should, in writing of something else, take notice of the passages objected to and explain them. It seems that Newman may have been putting this advice into practice by his use of his appendix to *The Arians*. He states the three points at issue as:

1) that 'there was a temporary suspense of the functions of the "Ecclesia docens"';
2) that 'the body of the Bishops failed in their confession of the faith';
3) that 'general councils, etc., said what they should not have said, or did what obscured and compromised revealed truth'.

1) By this, Newman was not seeking to deny that the Council of Nicaea of the year 325 had effectively defined and promulgated the dogma of Our Lord's divinity everywhere and for all time. He did not dispute that the dogma would have become known to the faithful throughout Christendom both because of the fame of the Council and the teaching of its great champions such as Athanasius and Hilary. What he had meant by the word 'suspense' (which he had used purposely in preference to 'suspension') was that from Nicaea until the Council of Constantinople in 381 'there was no authoritative utterance of the Church's infallible voice in the matter', or, to use his original words in the *Rambler*, 'there was nothing after Nicaea of firm, unvarying, consistent testimony for nearly sixty years.' He was stating this as historical fact.

2) That 'the *body* of Bishops failed in their confession of faith'. He had not used the word 'body' in the sense of the Latin 'corpus' as used in theological treatises (and it was the Latin translation which had come before the

authorities in Rome). If that had been his meaning then, he conceded, his statement would certainly be heretical. His meaning had been 'the great preponderance' or 'the mass'. Again, he points out, he is stating an historical fact. In support of this he cites St Gregory Nazianzen as saying that to subscribe to Arianism was one of the requisites for entering, or remaining in, the episcopate. There were those who seemed for a while invincible but at last succumbed. Even if, in spirit, they did not fall into heresy, they did, by signing, consent to it. Few escaped, but God at last saw to it that there remained 'some seed and some root to bring about the reflowering of Israel.'

3) That '*general* Councils said what they should not have said, and did what obscured and compromised revealed truth.' The question here is what is meant by the word 'general'. By 'general' he did not mean 'ecumenical'; if he had, that would indeed have been unworthy of a Catholic. But he could not have been referring to ecumenical Councils since none were held during the years in question. He cites St Robert Bellarmine [theologian Archbishop of Milan and Doctor of the Church] as dividing 'general councils' into four groups, one of which was 'reprobate'; it was in that group that Bellarmine placed the Arian councils. These, comments Newman, were large enough to be called 'general'. He concludes: 'When I spoke of "general councils compromising revealed truth", I spoke of the Arian or Eusebian Councils, not of the Catholic.'[34]

Newman's Historical View

At the root of the disapproval which Newman met with in his presentation of the shortcomings of the bishops during the Arian crisis, and which led to his delation to Rome, was a misunderstanding of the type of theology he was employing. His critics thought he was tampering with the theological principles which govern the Church's teaching office; that is, they assumed that he was writing in a dogmatic sense, whereas what he was doing was merely describing the facts of an historical situation. In the Appendix to the third edition of *The Arians,* referred to above, he explained that in contrasting the ineffectuality of the bishops with the staunchness of the laity, he had not intended to contradict Catholic teaching on the infallibility of the *Ecclesia docens,*

> But on that occasion I was writing simply historically, not doctrinally, and, while it is historically true, it is in no sense doctrinally false, that a Pope, as a private doctor and much more Bishops, when not teaching formally, may err, as we find they did err in the fourth century.[35]

Congar in *Lay People* expresses reservations about Newman's treatment of the fidelity of the laity in contrast to the failures of the hierarchy. He says that *On Consulting the Faithful* can be misleading if it is taken as a complete account of the Arian crisis: it deals with only one aspect of it, often using the texts of lay historians who favoured the laity. He adds that this aspect was nevertheless real and has been so recognized by 'other able Catholic historians.' He agrees that the people's resistance to Arianism throughout the fourth century is unquestionable; it was a heresy of intellectuals often accepted by the bishops themselves. He remarks that 'the Church's central magisterium was not very active' at that time (and mentions in passing that there were those who found in that circumstance an objection to papal infallibility).[36]

Newman's comments in the appendix to *The Arians* mentioned above goes a long way towards mitigating any over-emphasis there may be on the fidelity of the laity such as Congar has remarked on. In it, Newman affirms that, of course, 'there were great and illustrious exceptions' to episcopal failures. He names, *inter alios*, Athanasius, Hilary, Basil, the two Gregorys and Ambrose. There were, too, exceptions to the Christian heroism of the laity, especially in some of the great towns. He reminds us that when speaking of the laity he includes their 'parish priests' (so to call them); 'but on the whole', he adds, 'taking a wide view of history, we are obliged to say that the governing body of the Church came short, and the governed were pre-eminent in faith, zeal, courage, and constancy.'[37] There is often a kind of forensic ardour in Newman's manner which may have contributed to an impression that his argument on behalf of the laity is overdone.[38]

Chapter Seven

The *Sensus Fidelium* and Opposition to the Magisterium

The Universal Moral Law and the Christian Sense

An attempt will be made in this chapter to apply Newman's teaching on the *sensus fidelium* to the situation where a large proportion of the laity are found to be in opposition to the magisterium in a judgement on a certain moral matter. The moral matter in question is the declaration contained in the papal encyclical, *Humanae Vitae*, in reiteration of the Church's authoritative teaching, that 'each and every marriage act (quilibet matrimonii usus) must remain open to the transmission of life.' It directed that any practice intended to render the conjugal act infecund was to be absolutely excluded as a licit means of regulating birth. The encyclical explains the basis of that teaching as being 'founded upon the inseparable con-nection, willed by God and unable to be broken by man on his own initiative, between the two meanings of the conjugal act: the unitive meaning and the procreative meaning.'[1] It has been claimed that this teaching is not supported by the *sensus fidelium*, inasmuch as it has met with opposition in the faithful. Thus, it is being said that the sense of the faithful judges that to deprive the conjugal act of its openness to the transmission of life is, or in some cases may be, licit.

Universal Application of Moral Law

A problem in relation to the *sensus fidelium* as applied to a moral question, as distinct from an article of faith, presents itself at the outset. This is that the moral law is discernible by, and binding on, everyone, Christian and non-Christian. 'The natural law [which expresses the original moral sense], present in the heart of each man and established by reason, is universal in its precepts and its authority extends to all men.'[2] That being so, what scope, or need, is there, in the moral sphere, for a supernatural discernment, present only in the Mystical Body of Christ, and intrinsic to the Christian faith; a sense, as we have heard Möhler explain it, 'eminently Christian', the outcome of the action of the Holy Spirit in the Church?

It is undeniable that there is an especial need in this day and age for an evangelical discernment in a question which concerns marriage and sexuality. The views and practices of the world in this area are not only markedly opposed to the Gospel. They are supported 'by the powerful and pervasive organization of the means of social communication, which subtly endanger freedom and the capacity for objective judgement.'[3] A specially Christian orientation, to be found in the *sensus fidelium*, is therefore of great importance in the present era. A complete answer to the question as to how the *sensus fidelium* can be applicable to the Christian moral life, seeing that moral laws are universally knowable, would require a whole study of its own. It is the intention here to eschew generalities and concentrate on the particular, concrete matter that has been specified at the beginning of this chapter.

The Christian Perception

If we take first, in Newman's exposition of the *sensus fidelium*, the central idea that it is a sort of instinct in the Mystical Body, a sense, 'eminently Christian', we are led to ask this question: What is there that is 'eminently Christian' in the attitude of the Mystical Body towards sexuality in marriage, an attitude which could not be shared by strangers to the Gospel and its interpretation by the successors of the Apostles? It must be borne in mind at this point that the rejection of artificial means of birth regulation as immoral has not been, until recent years, the preserve of the Catholic Church. Within the memory of persons now living there was, before contraception became generally practised and morally acceptable in the West, and areas of the world under western influence, an almost universal sense, a sense which needed to be battled against by the early promoters of scientific means of contraception, that it was indecent and wrongful. What, then, is there in the Christian idea of marriage, an idea which encompasses the procreative act, and is so beyond the extra-Christian perception that only a sense inherent in the Mystical Body could be capable of the idea?

We recall once more, remembering Newman's quotation from Möhler, how this Christian sense cannot be separated from the Christian truths from and by which it is formed. We saw how several of the post-Vatican II theologians who have reflected on the *sensus fidelium* were also at pains to show that it is intrinsic to faith. Following these perceptions, we can say that, in order for there to be an authentic exercise of the sense of the Christian community in the sphere of conjugal morality, the people's belief and understanding in this sphere must be worthy of the quality and depth of the word of the Gospel relating to it. There is reason to doubt that such a belief and understanding exists widely at present in the faithful. Without that profundity, and a strong evangelical foundation, the 'sense of the faith' is incapable of standing up to the contrary influence of the world. In the words of Pope John Paul: 'It is not sufficient that [*Humanae Vitae*] be faithfully and fully proposed but it also is necessary to devote oneself to demonstrating its deepest reasons.'[4] Have these deep reasons been proposed to and assimilated by the faithful so devotedly that a Christian *phronēma* in this regard has been formed in them? Before this point is dealt with further, let us dispose of the question of what importance is to be attributed to a majority view found in the faithful.

The *Sensus Fidelium* as a Majority View

A majority which, with apparent justification, is often claimed to be enjoyed by the opponents of *Humanae Vitae*, does not necessarily signify the operation of the *sensus fidelium*, since 'The "supernatural sense of faith" ... does not consist solely or necessarily in the consensus of the faithful. Following Christ, the Church seeks the truth which is not always the same as the majority opinion.'[5] Aidan Nichols, on the question of establishing the beliefs of the greater part, the *maior pars* of the faithful, considers that 'What is at stake is not the counting of heads so much as the weighing of testimonies. What we are concerned with is a *pars* which is *maior* because it is *sanior*, the better-judging and thus weightier part of the Christian people.' Considering the question as to how this *sanior pars* is to be identified, Nichols finds two leads, one in Ullathorne, as cited by Newman, the other in Newman himself. Ullathorne had written in connection with the definition of the doctrine of the Immaculate Conception:

> The more devout the faithful grew, the more devoted they showed themselves towards this mystery. And it is the devout who have the surest instinct in discerning the mysteries of which the Holy Spirit breathes the grace through the Church and who, with as sure a tact, reject what is alien to her teaching.

This leaves open the question as to who are the devout, but would clearly exclude, Nichols thinks, those not practising their faith regularly or not sharing the already defined faith of the Church. Those who lead manifestly holy lives and whose love of God is shown in love of neighbour give the best testimony. Nichols adds that the lives of the acknowledged saints play a considerable part in the obtaining of the *sensus fidelium*. Thus, we note that it is not only the contemporary faithful who must be listened to. This prompts us to reflect, as Newman would remind us, that the Church does not consist only of the Church militant.

The second indication referred to by Nichols occurs in *On Consulting* where Newman argues that the voice of the faithful during the struggle for Nicene orthodoxy comes to us with added emphasis when we consider that their loyal perseverance in bearing witness to the tradition of the Apostles involved persecution in life, limb and property; that is to say, that the witness which should be taken the most seriously is that which entails suffering. Nichols expresses the point thus: 'It is those whose Christian discipleship is costing, yet who stick to what they believe through thick and thin, who should be most listened to by the theologian concerned to hear the authentic accents of Tradition.'[6]

There have certainly been, and possibly still are, many heroic sufferers in the cause of chaste wedlock; for example, by the incurring of comparative poverty, even scorn, in the affluent society, by having to do battle against the structures and social and medical mores of the age, even by impairment of the mother's health. Surely such as they merit the most attentive hearing. On what grounds must their testimony give way to that of the opponents, in word or deed, of apostolic teaching? Amid all the wide consultation which took place prior to Paul VI's affirmation of the Church's teaching, surely their testimony must have been taken and heeded. Thus, the *sensus fidelium* on contraception, if indeed it has functioned and been acknowledged, may already have been found in holiness of life and in adherence to apostolic teaching prior to the onset of the rejection which greeted *Humanae Vitae*.

The Sacramentality of Marriage: The Teaching of Pope John Paul II

If we seek to identify what it is which supplies the 'eminently Christian' perception in relation to the morality or otherwise of contraception, we are drawn instantly to contemplate the existence of marriage as one of the sacraments of the Church and to see where that leads us. The sacramentality of marriage has scarcely entered into the contraception debate; this in spite of the fact that *Casti Connubii*, the most important papal statement on the subject prior to *Humanae Vitae*, and much referred to by the later document, opened with an assertion of its sacramental rank. Nor has it yet in the least been acknowledged that, in raising marriage to the rank of a sacrament of the New Law, Christ thereby 'entrusted the entire regulation and care of it to His Bride the Church.'[7] We think of it, once the ceremony is over, as a private matter. Yet we have been asked by Pope John Paul to reflect on the liturgical character of the use of marriage.[8] An effort in that direction will be made later in this chapter.

Marriage then, being a sacrament, what, if any, sacramental status or character is consequently to be accorded to the marriage act? As things are at present, catechesis has not, generally speaking, dwelt much upon this point; not, that is to say, until that given by Pope John Paul II who, during a series of general audiences held between September 1979 and November 1984, showed us how to locate human sexuality within the mystery of the incarnate Word. This teaching has not so far been the subject of general study in the Church. Yet it would seem that it is to such instruction that the Christian communion must respond if it is to acquire a view of marriage and sexuality which makes it capable of bearing a unique Christian witness in this field.

In an address of 18 July 1984, part of a series of 'Reflections on *Humanae Vitae*', Pope John Paul, in remarking how the norm of *Humanae Vitae* 'concerns all men', adds:

> All the more does it concern all believers and members of the Church, since the reasonable character of this norm indirectly finds confirmation and solid support in the sum total of the theology of the body ... The norm of the natural law, based on [the] ethos [of the redemption of the body]

finds not only a new expression, but also a fuller anthropological and ethical foundation in the word of the Gospel and in the purifying and corroborating action of the Holy Spirit.

He then proposes that every believer and especially every theologian should 'reread and ever more deeply understand the moral doctrine of the encyclical in this complete context.'[9]

The series of papal audiences referred to (which included the address from which quotations have been given above) constitutes a catechesis on the bodily dimension of human personhood, sexuality and marriage in the light of biblical revelation. These are published under the title *The Theology of the Body* with the sub-title *Human Love in the Divine Plan*. The principal texts John Paul uses are from Genesis (2:24), Ephesians (5:21–33), Matthew (19) and Mark (10). Do we find in these addresses what, in particular, we are looking for, which is: Does the late Pope clearly say, or say something which allows us to deduce, that he regards the conjugal act as partaking of the sacramental character and status of marriage itself? (Statements made in a papal audience are cited here not as having a binding, but a strongly persuasive authority.) It seems to us that unless the conjugal act does arrive at such status in developed Christian belief then there can be no exclusively Christian sense with regard to it, or anything relating to it, for example, birth control. The Pope does not disappoint our expectations. A perception of the conjugal act as indeed being implicated in the sacramentality of marriage, though it is obvious *passim*, emerges in particular from what he says about the sacramental sign.

Before he comes to that stage in his addresses, he has

spoken of marriage as a primordial sacrament and situated it as the central point of the 'Sacrament of Creation'.[10] It eventually becomes an integral part of the new sacramental economy in Christ. Pope John Paul sees the most essential feature of Christian marriage as being an image of the mystical union between Christ and His Church. Reverence for Christ is the basis of the relationship between the spouses.[11] So what is required at the outset of this 'rereading and deeper understanding' of *Humanae Vitae* urged on us is reflection on what implications that doctrine has for the practice of birth control. So far, such consideration has not been to the fore in discussion of the subject.

I am concerned here with one particular aspect of the mystical union of which marriage is an image, namely, the aspect of liturgy to which John Paul draws attention. Speaking of marriage as a determinate liturgical action proper to the Church, the Pope sets out to show how what he terms the 'language of the body'[12] is 'the substratum and content of the sacramental sign of spousal communion'.[13] Marriage is a sacrament which is contracted by means of the words spoken by the couple; it is by reason of their content that the words are a sign: 'I take you as my wife-as my husband', and the promise of lifelong love and fidelity. The words *per se* are merely the sign of the coming into being of the marriage which at this point has not yet been constituted in its full reality. The words can be fulfilled only by conjugal intercourse. The address continues:

> Thus then, from the words whereby the man and the woman express their willingness to become 'one flesh'[14] according to the eternal truth established in the mystery of creation, we pass to the reality which corresponds to these words. Both

the one and the other element are important in regard to the structure of the sacramental sign.[15]

Thus John Paul clearly places the physical consummation of the marriage, since it is one of the aspects which constitute the marriage 'in its full reality', firmly in the sacramental context; not only that, but as belonging to the sacramental sign as surely as do the words spoken at the altar. This allows us to regard the physical marriage act as not simply sacramental but as belonging specifically to the nuptial and sacramental rite. Nor does it seem, from what John Paul says in a certain later address, that the link with the marriage rite is borne by the initial act of consummation only but by every subsequent performance of it.

In this later address, entitled 'The Language of the Body and the Spirituality of Marriage', the Pope, returning to the fifth chapter of Ephesians, points out that the text brings a mystical dimension to the 'language of the body'. It says of marriage, 'This is a great mystery' (Eph. 5:32). This mystery is fulfilled in the spousal union between Christ and his Church. 'Nevertheless,' the Pope continues, 'the author of Ephesians[16] does not hesitate to extend the analogy of Christ's union with the Church in spousal love ... to the sacramental sign of the matrimonial pact between man and woman, who "defer to one another out of reverence for Christ" (Eph. 5:21). He [the author of Ephesians] does not hesitate to extend that mystical analogy to the "language of the body" reread in the truth of the spousal love and the conjugal union of the two.' The Pope goes on to speak of how the sacraments penetrate the soul and body, the masculinity and femininity of the personal subject [for 'male and female created he them'], with the power of sanctity, and that this is expressed and brought about by the language of the liturgy. He continues:

> The liturgy, liturgical language, elevates the conjugal pact of man and woman, based on the language of the body reread in truth, to the dimensions of mystery. At the same time it enables that pact to be fulfilled in these dimensions through the language of the body.[17]

He asserts that the sacramental sign signifies not only the *fieri* (the 'becoming') of the marriage but builds its whole *esse* (its 'being'), its duration. He explains how the 'language of the body' is 'an uninterrupted continuity of liturgical language':

> It [the sign of the sacrament] signifies both the one and the other [that is, both the 'becoming' and the 'being'] as a sacred and sacramental reality, rooted in the dimension of the covenant and grace in the dimension of creation and redemption. In this way, the liturgical language assigns to both, to the man and to the woman, love, fidelity and conjugal honesty through the language of the body. It assigns them the unity and the indissolubility of marriage in the language of the body. It assigns them as a duty all the *sacrum* (holy) of the person and of the communion of persons, and likewise their femininity and masculinity – precisely in this language.[18]

The Pope goes on to explain further how the sacramental sign builds the whole being and duration of the marriage:

> In this sense we affirm that liturgical language becomes the language of the body. This signifies a series of acts and duties which form the spirituality of marriage, its ethos. In the daily lives of the spouses these acts become duties, and the duties become acts. These acts – as also the

commitments – are of a spiritual nature. Nevertheless, they are expressed at the same time with the language of the body ... The 'language of the body', as an uninterrupted continuity of liturgical language is expressed not only as the attraction and mutual pleasure of the Song of Songs, but also as a profound experience of the *sacrum* (the holy).[19]

To hear Pope John Paul II speak of the conjugal act as liturgical language gives us the confidence to bind its use, in domesticity, to the first, ritualistic coming into being of the marriage at the altar. So what does this mean for the *sensus fidelium* in relation to the conjugal act and to the permissibility or otherwise, of contraception? We have seen how John Paul's analysis makes us able to say that the marriage act relates back to the initial rite. The imbued Christian sense would perceive this liturgical significance in the conjugal act inasmuch as it would be aware of a link with the altar. To appreciate this would make the faithful apprehensive lest an interference with the conjugal act would be akin to sacrilege, which might carry them to the point where they did indeed perceive such interference as irreverence to Christ. Along with this would go the fear lest such interference would prejudice the original authenticity of the rite.

I should explain why I have placed emphasis on the rite of Christian marriage in the search for the place to which a special Christian perception of marriage would attach itself. The reason is that prior to, and later, outside of, the Christian dispensation, marriage is not without a sacramental character. In man's state of innocence it was a primordial sacrament, and even after that continued to be the figure of the 'great mystery' of which St Paul speaks. It is the rite, and what the rite carries with it, which constitutes marriage a sacrament proper to the Church.

A second reason why the rite is thought to be so important to the present study is that a rite is a procedure which has to take a prescribed form in order to be effective. This leads to the question: Could a lack of integrity in the conjugal act, that is, the use of contraception, afflict in some way the validity of the ritual which forms marriage? Of course a marriage once consummated by an integral sexual act could not be rendered invalid by a subsequent contracepted one; yet it would be hard to say that the contracepted act with its failure to observe the requirements of the ritual, with its compromising of the procreative element, would have no deleterious effect. An act which, being of ritual character, but not observing the sacramental norm, surely 'does not work' in the sense that it cannot be taken up into the sacramental context. Since it does not work in sympathy with conjugal union, then must there not at least be considered the question as to whether it works against it? There is on record an instance of this consideration having been given. On the publication of *Humanae Vitae*, the late Bishop Cashman, the then Bishop of Arundel and Brighton, commented that, if what it said were true, then the use of contraception amounted to a putting asunder of man and wife, a kind of divorce.

It may be objected that deductions such as the foregoing belong to the realms of reflection and dissertation on the *sensus fidelium*, and that their conclusions are not to be looked for in that spontaneous, inward perception which is the *sensus fidelium* itself. We meet the objection by recalling Newman's distinction between the 'implicit' and the 'explicit' in human thought. It is not far-fetched to suppose that it could be 'implicit' in a truly Christianized attitude to marriage that married life in all its aspects should be perceived as having at all times an indefeasible link to the occasion of the marriage vows. Such an attitude would ensure the rejection of the idea of contraception through the deeply-seated instinct or *phronēma* of which Newman speaks as belonging to the *sensus fidelium*.

A Philosophical Foundation

So far our argument has been drawn from the requirements of sacramental ritual. But in this day and age when the attitudes of the world have so deeply permeated the Church, would it be practical to begin from that standpoint in seeking a truly Christian formation of the sense of the faithful in relation to the marriage act? How is inculcation on the lines of John Paul's theology of the body to be achieved over time and eventually taken aboard by the *sensus fidelium*? The Christian view, in order to withstand that of the world, and to be able to give a comprehensible account of itself to the world, must be coordinated with a compatible philosophy. The Church's teaching on the marital act needs to be preceded by and allied with the recognition that the married pair are faced with an objective ontological order in this act. The Christian needs to see that the authenticity of married love must be tested by whether it takes into account the real order of being and value which ultimately derives its authority from the first law-giving act of creation itself. It must be acknowledged that a couple cannot authentically substitute for the real order some order of their own making.[20] Regard must be had to pre-existent truth and the mind conformed to reality.

Unfortunately the prevalent philosophies of the age,

which have infected many members of the Church, do not recognize any inviolability in the natural structure of the marital act. Christians have come to be swayed by utilitarian considerations in their moral decisions which take no account of the real order of being. Added to this is a resultant antinomian attitude towards sexual behaviour that has gained much ground, not only in society at large but in the Church also, and is becoming the norm. In the face of this kind of morality, or lack of morality, any contention that the conjugal act has a spiritual connotation is considered to be an argument in support of contraception, not against it. Pope Paul VI, speaking of the phenomenon of 'a ravaging eroticism' in the world of today, related it to the 'distressful state of a materialistic civilization that has an obscure realization that in this mysterious domain is to be found, as it were, the last refuge of a sacred value'.[21]

To take a further example, not this time from the erotic atmosphere of the secular world but from would-be Catholic theology: There was published in the *New York Times* on 30 July 1968, beneath the signature of over two hundred theologians, a statement initiated by Fr Charles Curran, associate professor of theology at the Catholic University of America and Vice-President of the American Theological Society. The statement contended that in some circumstances contraception was permissible, even necessary, 'to preserve and foster the values and sacredness of marriage'. They justified their 'outspokenness' by pleading their 'true commitment to the mystery of Christ and the Church'.

Pope John Paul's Philosophical Approach

We turn to Pope John Paul again, this time to his pre-petrine writings, for the preparation of a congenial and fertile ground for the growth of the 'eminently Christian sense' of which Möhler speaks. There lies at the heart of Wojtyla's teaching on this subject a view which holds that sexuality in marriage always entails an entire self-giving if it is not to violate the dignity of the person. In this view:

> [S]exual intercourse in marriage has an inherent meaning of total bodily self-giving. Contraception overlays this meaning with a contradictory language of withholding and refusal. The fertility which is withheld or refused is not simply a superficial, biological component of the person which can be manipulated in the pursuit of other ends, but an aspect of the person as a whole. Contraception therefore violates the dignity of the person because it falsifies the total offering of self which intercourse is meant to express.[22]

The human person cannot unilaterally make a gift of himself to another in any way he chooses. He owes conformity to a pre-existent moral value, with which creation is infused. Wojtyla speaks of 'justice to the Creator' whose will is expressed in the order of being and value which natural law embodies. A being's nature is the source of all the dynamic tendencies seen in that being. Nature is not just the blind confluence of innate tendencies but rather represents design, purpose, intent. It is 'a law-giving act', and law is an act of reason and will, a dimension of a person. With this emphasis on the person, the Pope's philosophy counters the accusation which has often been made that the Church's teaching on contraception is based on a too narrowly 'physicalist' approach.[23]

Chapter Eight

A Last Reflection with Newman

I will give Newman the last word on the matters which, with his help, we have been discussing. Of course, the subject of contraception and its use in marriage, which occupied the preceding chapter, was not a thorny theological and philosophical problem in Newman's day because of the absence of the scientific methods now commonly employed and the fact that no movement had begun to argue for the permissibility of the practice. However, we do know something of his fundamental view of marriage. He saw it as a very great sacrifice in that it entailed such an utter surrender of freedom and such total availability to the spouse. He marvelled at its being undertaken. This view of marriage as a sacrifice has been, and doubtless still is, the view of the Church, though insistence on it is largely in abeyance as being entirely 'off-message' in the present climate. For example, the introduction to the marriage service in the old St Andrew missal, after referring to marriage as a sacrament instituted by Jesus Christ, and to the nuptial bond as the figure of the sacred union of Christ and his Church, goes on to compare marriage with the Eucharist in that each of them is at the same time both a sacrifice and a sacrament. The bridal pair, ministers to each other of the sacrament of marriage, are, so to speak, its priests and its victims alike.

Nowadays there has crept in 'a mistaken theoretical and practical concept of the independence of the spouses in relation to each other'.[1] This attitude, of course, is bolstered by the practice of contraception; in fact the practice is necessary to it. This teaching cannot, in the face of what we have learnt from Pope John Paul's addresses, be seen as peripheral as some have claimed it to be. We can now see, with the Pope's guidance, how, since the conjugal act has such spiritual importance and significance, a corresponding seriousness must be accorded to any interference with its integrity. The Pope speaks of the theology of the body and, as we have seen, places sexuality at the centre of creation and of the continuing Christian dispensation. When we see the legitimate expression of the sexual instinct so importantly placed as we have now seen it, it is understandable why the Church has regarded sexual sin as so serious. The gravity of her perception of the sin is consonant with the gravity of her approach to the legitimate action. The Church has been criticized for a negative attitude in this matter, of over-emphasizing the seriousness of offences against the Sixth Commandment. Well, those who have brought these charges have succeeded of late years in almost completely silencing the clergy with regard to that commandment.

Newman, in common with all the saints,[2] regarded sexual purity as being at the centre of the Christian life. This is in accordance with evangelical doctrine. As Raniero Cantalamessa remarks: '[T]he ideal of purity holds a privileged place in every synthesis on Christian morality in the New Testament. We could say that there isn't a Letter of St Paul's in which he doesn't dedicate space to it when he describes the new life in the Spirit.'[3]

With the glossing over of the wrongfulness of contraception which has taken place, the whole area of the wrong use of sexuality has come to be excepted from the moral field, as logically had to happen. Not only that, but morality itself has been edged away from the mainstream of Christian thought and exhortation. Moral consciousness nowadays concentrates on large, rather de-personalized and global wrongdoing, 'the sin situation'. It attaches itself to the sort of sins for which governments, civilizations and supermarkets can be blamed rather than the individual. The promotion of this type of sin-ethos has the effect of robbing the Christian faith and Christian life of their tone and rigour.

Newman saw Christian belief as having been arrived at in the early days of the Church through gradual elevation of personal morality. In presenting the arguments for the existence of God which have prevailed in human experience, Newman gives prominence to moral experience and the awareness of moral obligation. The justification for religious belief was a subject close to Newman's heart throughout his life. He was concerned to examine the mental processes by which a person becomes a believer or an unbeliever. He regarded conscience as the great internal teacher of religion. He did not confine experiential awareness of God to the moral life, but, if he had to look for proof of there being a God, that is where he would look for it. He declares:

> Conscience does not repose on itself but vaguely reaches
> forward to something beyond self, and dimly discerns a
> sanction higher than self for its decisions ... And hence it
> is that we are accustomed to speak of conscience as a voice,
> ... and moreover a voice, or the echo of a voice, imperative
> and constraining, like no other dictate in the whole of our

experience ... If, as is the case, we feel responsibility, are ashamed, are frightened, at transgressing the voice of conscience, this implies that there is One to whom we are responsible, before whom we are ashamed, whose claims upon us we fear ... If the cause of these emotions does not belong to this visible world, the Object to which [our] perception is directed must be Supernatural and Divine; and thus the phenomena of Conscience, as a dictate, avail to impress the imagination with the picture of a Supreme Governor, a Judge, holy, just, powerful, all-seeing, retributive, and are the creative principle of religion ...[4]

Certainly, as far as the Christian religion is concerned, it cannot be denied that sin is at the centre of the salvation message. Christ came to save us from our sins. In Ronald Lawler's words, 'The moral implications of Jesus' message are so central to it that they appear prominently in the original proclamation of the Gospel; they appear in the heavily moral emphasis of the early Pauline epistles as they do in all later Catholic teaching.'[5] The fact that St Paul is so little invoked in current moral debate ought to raise our suspicions of the Christian value of opposition to the traditional moral teaching of the Church.

Newman regarded the moral argument as the best philosophical argument for religion. In the last chapter of his *Grammar of Assent* he avers that the feeling of guilt is the basis of natural religion which 'is founded one way or other on the sense of sin; and without that vivid sense it would hardly have any precepts or any observances.' Another reason Newman has for stressing the moral argument is how strikingly absent God appears from his world. Why does God not give us more immediate knowledge of himself? 'Why is it possible without absurdity to deny His will, His attributes, His existence? ... He is specially "a hidden God"; and with our best efforts we can only glean from the surface of the world some faint and fragmentary views of Him.'[6] The sight of the world is nothing else than the prophet's scroll, full of 'lamentations, and mourning, and woe'. The answer to this 'profound mystery, which is absolutely beyond human solution' is for Newman that 'either there is no Creator, or this living society of men is in a true sense discarded from His presence.'[7]

It should be said, since Newman has been criticized on this point, that although he regards the moral argument from conscience as integral and basic to theism of any kind, yet he is aware of the basis for belief in a personal God. For example, that man's affections, in the exercise of which lies the happiness of the human soul, require something more vast and enduring than anything created; so that 'here is at once a reason for saying that the thought of God, and nothing short of it, is the happiness of man.'[8]

Can Newman's View of the *Sensus Fidelium* Support Dissent?

We saw above (in Chapter 6) how Newman speaks of five ways in which the consensus of the faithful bears upon the manifestation of the tradition of the Church. The first of these is a testimony to the fact of the apostolic dogma. For Ullathorne and Newman 'the universal conviction of pious Catholics' is 'the faithful reflection of the pastoral teaching'. Through the ages, the Church's teaching on contraception has been consistently against it.[9] *Humanae Vitae* maintains and enlarges upon that tradition. The Apostles and their successors teach in the name of Christ and with his authority. It cannot be regarded as a merely conventional preamble, something that the Supreme Pontiff would be expected to say, when Paul VI declares in his encyclical, 'We now intend, by virtue of the mandate entrusted to Us by Christ, to give our reply to these grave questions.' The contestation which followed arose because of the expectation of an earthly solution from the seat of the Vicar of Christ. What did emerge was a teaching which evinced the divinely guided instinct for supernatural truth in the Mystical Body of Christ. That instinct Newman names as the second feature of the *sensus fidelium*.

The third of the ways in which Newman regards the *sensus fidelium* is as the direction of the Holy Spirit. Aidan Nichols sees a problem in connection with this point. He is not dealing with any particular doctrine of faith or morals but is speaking generally when he writes:

> Today, it is difficult to know whether fluctuations in the *sensus fidelium* are the result of the activity of the Holy Spirit, leading the Church into all truth, or the effect of the corrosion of specifically Christian meanings, truths, and values by the spirit of the age – a spirit not unconnected with what the New Testament calls the 'prince of this world'.[10]

A person who experienced, and now reflects upon, the virulent character of the birth control movement prior to *Humanae Vitae* and the contemptuous spirit in which it was received in many quarters, would have serious doubts concerning the influence of the Holy Spirit in its rejection. Charity, joy, peace, patience, gentleness, faithfulness and modesty, for example, qualities traditionally listed by the Church as the fruits of that Spirit, were seldom to be found in the lay branch of the dissenting movement. Karl Rahner, a leading instigator of his fellow clergy in the path of dissent, advised the laity to avoid 'scornful criticism and unbridled insults [the laity being in fact engaged in that manner] and to form their consciences'.[11] Of course, as Rahner implies, conscience has to be formed. In view of his example of opposition to *Humanae Vitae*, one supposes that he contemplates the possibility of a lay person's conscience also leading in that direction. But how would it be possible for a Catholic conscience, duly formed in accordance with the constant teaching of the Church, now confirmed and developed by the Supreme Pontiff, to be at variance with that teaching? Yet at the time when Pope Paul VI's encyclical appeared there was much talk of following one's conscience with the implication that the process might serve as some kind of escape clause. As for the *sensus fidelium*, it would not be possible for its genuine exercise to go contrary to revelation and to apostolic teaching which stems from revelation, the revelation in this case being of the kind which comes through the observable facts of nature. What was plainer to see than the working of the *sensus fidelium* in all the contumely and arrogance of that time was the loss of the *pietas fidei*. Newman never advocated the 'ecclesiastical prohibition to doubt and enquire' as a means of preserving belief but, commenting on the fact that loss of faith did occur among Catholics, he observed:

> A Catholic is kept from scepticism ... by admiration, trust and love. While he admires, trusts, and loves our Lord and His Church, these feelings prohibit him from doubt; they guard and protect his faith; the real prohibition is from within. But suppose those feelings go ...[12]

The fourth of the ways in which Newman saw the *sensus*

fidelium in its testimony to the tradition of the Church was as an answer to the prayer of the Mystical Body. The wrongfulness of contraception is capable of being perceived by the world at large and, in the past, has been perceived; it does not, like the mysteries of the Christian faith, have 'its birth in that people which is ruled by the Holy Ghost'. However, the prayer of the Mystical Body is much needed in order to bring about a full Christian understanding of the 'deepest reasons' behind *Humanae Vitae*.

The fifth characteristic of the operation of the *sensus fidelium* according to Newman was 'jealousy of error'. A spontaneous rejection of error as being alien to their creed can hardly be said of the attitude of the faithful towards the Church's teaching on birth control; rather, it was our reaction to *Humanae Vitae* which showed a response so like jealousy of error that it has been mistaken for the genuine thing. But the jealousy of error element does not exist on its own; it is present in alliance with the other attributes of the *sensus fidelium*. Aidan Nichols, in urging the need for the revival of doctrinal consciousness in our time, makes this point in the following terms:

> [W]hat has happened to that 'jealousy of error', that instinctive repugnance toward heresy so crucial for John Henry Newman in his account of the *consensus fidelium*? That jealousy of error was, for Newman, but the other side of the medal to 'instinct' for supernatural truth, 'direction' by the Holy Spirit and divine response to the prayer of the Christian people for right faith. Only as all of these – negative abreactions and positive attractions – together does the 'consensus fidelium' furnish its testimony to the fact of the apostolic teaching.[13]

Newman and the 'Real'

One of the main preoccupations of Newman's mind was with the 'real' as opposed to the 'unreal'. He believed that ideas of the mind had to be connected with concrete archetypes in order to be true. Mental reflections have real correlates in the universe or in that body of knowledge we possess by means of supernatural revelation endorsed by apostolic authority. The unreal is what does not correspond to what is in either world. Ian Ker comments on this preoccupation: 'Newman's ... lifelong concern to reconcile the ideal and the theoretical with the actual and the concrete, without sacrificing either, finds expression with that preoccupation with the "real" which runs through his writings and colours all his thought.'[14] The importance of this quality in Newman lies in the contrast it provides with the prevailing liberalism of his age which, of course, is even more prevalent in ours. It is one of the marks of liberalism to seek and be content with verbal constructs detached from the actuality and the object which is being spoken of. It is a case of the substitution of words for things. Liberalism of the kind which Newman opposed, and did so by setting against it his 'whole mind', is not concerned to present an objective truth. Among other ways, it shows itself, in the contraception argument, by proposals of a 'let's say this' or 'let's say that' kind, whereby a bogus solution to a difficulty is presented and a foot-in-either-camp style of peacemaking is on show. The 'real' has been one of the chief casualties of the contraception debate and this not only at the hands of the opponents of *Humanae Vitae* but equally of those who accept it or believe themselves to do so. Of all the aspects of Newman's thought, this emphasis on the 'real' is the one which could be applied the most profitably to the debate in question.

The most common argument (to the extent that any argument still continues, seeing that, after the first furore which greeted it, *Humanae Vitae* was laid quietly to rest), and the one which holds, or has held, the field is this: A distinction must be made between the objective evil which lies in contraception and its subjective wrongfulness, that is, the accountability of the person employing it. This is a mainstream theological approach and, though one among others with the same defect, it illustrates particularly well that detachment from the object which is to be found in most comments on *Humanae Vitae* and the practice of contraception. These comments dissociate themselves from both the concrete, physical substance of the contracepted act and from the subjective, mental element which is a component of it. They purport to make a clever and subtle distinction between the two elements but, in fact, they try to separate two things which are inseparable. Or rather, they take very little account of either. At the height of the discussion which followed in the wake of *Humanae Vitae*, appeal would sometimes be made to the analogy of the criminal law of homicide with its well-known variations of culpability (for example between murder and manslaughter) in cases where a person causes the death of another. The moral gravity in the use of contraception varies, it is argued, from case to case and from person to person. Thus, there is often, some would say probably always, a reduction in the degree of culpability, a reduction which may even take it to vanishing point.

In fact, a study of the law's maxim 'Actus non facit reum nisi mens sit rea' (An act does not make a person guilty of his crime unless the mind be also guilty) would be very apt and useful in showing up the falsity of the arguments in question and encourage a much-needed 'clearness of head, accuracy, scholarlike precision' which, for Newman, were qualities of 'the well-formed mind'.[15] Let it suffice here to say that the *actus reus* of the law is the material result of a person's conduct (e.g. in murder it is the death) and that the *mens rea* is the mental attitude of the wrongdoer towards that result. For example, some who kill intend that their conduct shall bring about the death, as in murder, while others kill with recklessness regarding the result of their conduct, as in the case of one who causes death by dangerous driving. This means that we must look first at what is the concrete outcome of the employment of contraception, that is, what is the *actus reus*.

Realizing that the *actus reus* of wrongdoing is not an activity but an accomplished deed, a state of affairs, we know for a start at least what the *actus reus* of contraception is not. It is not the swallowing of a contraceptive pill or the application of some mechanical device. We must advert to the outcome of that activity which consists of the performance of the conjugal act with the use of contraception. The *actus reus* is that outcome, and that outcome is a conjugal act which has been intentionally deprived of its openness to the transmission of life. The intention in the case of this offence is part of the *actus reus*, being a necessary constituent of the wrongful deed itself. Thus we have looked at the concrete, physical substance of the offence, together with its clear-cut subjective component. We have paid close attention to its specific character. This is what is rarely done when the rights and wrongs of contraception are talked about. The nature and quality of the wrongful act is taken little account of. Nor is the subjective component of the offence which lies in contraception squarely looked at. The prevalent notion that there must be some subjective element which somehow or other, who knows, absolves, or partly absolves the person concerned is completely unfocused and overlooks the 'resident' element of intention.

A further false argument is shown up by this calling in of the criminal law. This law shows that offences cannot be spoken of as if they were interchangeable; each offence has its own *actus reus* and its own *mens rea*. That consideration enables us to see, by analogy, that it is a mistake to treat offences against the moral law as though they were interchangeable; for example, just as there could arise circumstances which would make theft justifiable, so it is with contraception. Or, the Church has changed her mind, so it is claimed, on usury, so the practice of contraception may well, as time goes on, benefit from the same process. One cannot speak of procreation as though it were on a par with the activities of the stock exchange.

But the most cogent illustration of all that the reality of the offence is not being treated of in these arguments is the absence of any concern as to what is, or may be, the spiritual result of a vitiated conjugal act. Does not the Christian regard the spiritual as being the principle even of his bodily life? In fact, the Church has considered herself able to pronounce on the existence of a concomitant spiritual result of a wilfully incomplete conjugal act, saying that the result is the loss of the grace of God. We too carelessly assume that the Church no longer categorizes sins as either mortal, to denote a sin which deprives one of communion with God, or venial, a sin which does not entail that result. Much has been made of the absence from *Humanae Vitae* of the expression 'mortal (or grave) sin'. The encyclical was not addressed exclusively to those in communion with the Apostolic See but to all men of good will most of whom would be unfamiliar with Catholic terminology. There is sufficient sense of gravity conveyed by its section on 'Faithfulness to God's Design' to make any categorizing unnecessary. What of this passage from §13: 'To use this divine gift destroying, even if only partially, its meaning and its purpose is to contradict the nature both of man and of woman and of their most intimate relationship, and therefore it is to contradict also the plan of God and His will'?

While ever the Church is concerned with the result, the material combined with the spiritual, of wrongful conduct, she is unlikely to abandon the distinction between grave and venial sin. By all means let us cease to use the term mortal sin if we would be more comfortable without it, though that must be a flimsy gain which comes to us by discarding a word when the reality behind it is still there. It may act as a sop to muddled modern thought which sees in the term a lack of Christian compassion towards one's fellow sinner. But the question is, where does true compassion lie? It does not lie in these false, verbal solutions. A Christian concern for the married state and the true happiness of those who live in it would at least be asking certain neglected questions. For example, seeing that there is an inseparable connection in the will of God between the unitive and the procreative meaning of the conjugal act (if we are to believe *Humanae Vitae*), what effect on the matrimonial bond has the removal of the procreative meaning? Is it likely that the removal of the procreative meaning has no deleterious effects on marriage? What are these effects? The God of grace and the God of creation are one and the same. Therefore is it not to be feared that contraception, in severing me from the source of creation, severs me from the source of grace also? Compassion, once having looked at the matter in that light, would be likely to take the form of instruction in the 'deepest reasons' for the Church's teaching and exhortation to observe it. After all, there are licit though no less scientific methods of regulating birth. As was remarked earlier, when *Humanae Vitae* was first published, one of the English bishops of the time made the comment that, if what the encyclical said were true, it followed that contraception amounted to a putting asunder of man and wife. Rather than dismiss this comment with the curl of the lip that greeted it when first uttered, perhaps it is time now to consider whether contraception is, after all, a kind of divorce, whether it is destroying married oneness and, therefore, married love and happiness. Obviously, something is doing so. 'The energy of human intellect', to use a phrase of Newman's,[16] which is forever producing studies of the effects of this and that, has had little to say so far of the effects wrought on the marriage partnership by the practice of contraception. This itself is suspicious and suggests that there is an acknowledged awareness that the practice cannot bear scrutiny.

So far with contraception we have just, for the most part, contented ourselves with formulas and forms of words designed to skirt over this difficult matter and having nothing to do with physical or spiritual realities. To follow the suggestion of Pope John Paul II and 'reread in truth' the encyclical *Humanae Vitae*, would also be in accord with Newman's concern 'to reconcile the ideal and

the theoretical with the actual and the concrete without
sacrificing either.'

Conclusion

The *sensus fidelium* has its limits and these correspond to
the limits of the quality of faith, of the practice of the
faith and of moral observance. In recent years the climate
has become more favourable than it once was for 'the
rereading in truth' and deeper understanding of *Humanae
Vitae* such as has been called for by Pope John Paul.
Without such an understanding, the *sensus fidelium* in
relation to this aspect of marriage will not be sufficiently
informed to be worthy of the name. It will have to exhibit
all the five properties specified by Newman, which are:
Faithful witness to apostolic dogma; a supernatural
instinct proper to the Mystical Body; a direction of the
Holy Spirit; answer to the prayer of the Mystical Body;
jealousy of error, immediately felt as a scandal.

For a while after the publication of the encyclical, to
defend it in private was to run the risk of being thought
simple-minded, sexless or hard-hearted; to defend it in
public was to incite uproar. Worse, to defend it was not
intellectually respectable or *de rigueur*. Soon a veil of
silence was drawn over the subject and this is still,
generally speaking, in place. However, here and there, a
'*Humanae Vitae* was right' movement is now in existence
and gaining ground, as is the study of Pope John Paul's
'Theology of the Body'. This state of affairs raises the
hope that, in the fullness of time, by Catholics and by the
world at large, 'The Church of Rome will be found right
after all.'[17]

Abbreviations

Newman's Works

Newman collected his works in a uniform edition of 36 volumes (1868–81). Until his death in 1890 he continued making minor textual changes in reprints of individual volumes in this edition, of which all the volumes from 1886 were published by Longmans, Green and Co. of London. References to volumes in the uniform edition published after 1890 by Longmans are distinguished from other editions by the absence of publication details in parentheses after the title.

Apo.	*Apologia pro Vita Sua*, ed. Ian Ker (London: Penguin Books, 1994).
Ari.	*The Arians of the Fourth Century.*
Cons.	*On Consulting the Faithful in Matters of Doctrine*, ed. John Coulson (London: Geoffrey Chapman, 1961).
Dev.	*An Essay on the Development of Christian Doctrine.*
Diff. i, ii	*Certain Difficulties felt by Anglicans in Catholic Teaching*, 2 vols.
Ess. i, ii	*Essays Critical and Historical,* 2 vols.
GA	*An Essay in Aid of a Grammar of Assent*, ed. I. T. Ker (Oxford: Clarendon Press, 1985).

LD xi-xxxi   *The Letters and Diaries of John Henry Newman*, ed. Charles Stephen Dessain et al., vols xi-xxii (London: Nelson, 1961–72), xxiii-xxxi (Oxford: Clarendon Press, 1973–77).

PS i-viii   *Parochial and Plain Sermons*, 8 vols.

US   *Fifteen Sermons preached before the University of Oxford.*

VM   *The Via Media of the Anglican Church*, ed. H. D. Weidner (Oxford: Clarendon Press, 1990). The references are to Newman's preface to the third edition of *Lectures on the Prophetical Office of the Church*, renamed *Via Media*, i, and reprinted in Weidner's edition. (A second volume contained other articles and tracts by Newman written from 1833 until the end of his formal participation in the Oxford Movement.)

Works of Other Authors

Achiev.   Ian Ker, *The Achievement of John Henry Newman* (University of Notre Dame Press, 1991.)

CCC   *Catechism of the Catholic Church.*

Christi.   *The Vocation and the Mission of the Lay Faithful in the Church and in the World*: Post-Synodal Apostolic Exhortation *Christifideles Laici* of His Holiness John Paul II, 30 December 1988.

Concil.   J. B. Metz and E. Schillebeeckx (eds), *The*

	Teaching Authority of Believers [Concilium 180] (Edinburgh: T&T Clark, 1993).
Famil.	*The Role of the Christian Family in the Modern World (Familiaris Consortio)*: Apostolic Exhortation of Pope John Paul II, (1981).
Full.	Ian Ker, *Newman and the Fullness of Christianity*, (Edinburgh: T&T Clark, 1993).
HJ	This reference is to two essays by John J. Burkhard, *Sensus Fidei: Theological Reflection Since Vatican II:* I. 1965–1984; II.1985–1989 in The Heythrop Journal (1993) pp. 41–59 and 123–36.
Lawler	Ronald Lawler, Joseph M. Boyle, Jr, & William E. May, *Catholic Sexual Ethics* (Huntingdon, Indiana: Our Sunday Visitor, 1985).
Lay People	Yves Congar, *Lay People in the Church* (London: Geoffrey Chapman, 1957). The original French edition had appeared in 1953.
LG	Second Vatican Council's 'Dogmatic Constitution on the Church' (*Lumen Gentium*).
Shape	Aidan Nichols, *The Shape of Catholic Theology* (Edinburgh: T&T Clark, 1991).
TTB	John Paul II, *The Theology of the Body* (Boston, MA: Pauline Books & Media, 1997).

Notes

Ch. 1: Who Are 'the Faithful'? Why Do They Need a Sense of the Faith?

1. *Lay People*, 285–6.
2. Ibid. Footnote to 286 referring to J. Lebreton, 'Le désaccord de la foi populaire et de la théologie savante ...', in *Revue d'hist. ecclés.*, vol. xix (1923), 481–506, and vol. xx (1924), 5–37.
3. HJ 56.
4. *VM* 240.
5. *Dev*, 11–13, 27.
6. *Cons*. 73–4.
7. *CCC* §185–6.
8. *Lay People*, 288.

Ch. 2: Post-Vatican II Reflections on the *Sensus Fidelium*

1. See *Full*. 127–32.
2. *Achiev*. 96.
3. *Dev*. 173–7.
4. *Beyond the Prosaic*, ed. Stratford Caldecott (Edinburgh: T&T Clark, 1988), 164–5.
5. *Achiev*. 121.
6. HJ 41–59, 123–36.
7. *Concil*.
8. See HJ 58, note 1, for further comments by Burkhard on the usage of the two terms.
9. 'Sensus fidelium – Zeugnis in Kraft der Gemeinschaft', *Internationale katholische Zeitschrift 'Communio'* 16 (1987), 420–33. An English translation appeared the following year as '*Sensus fidelium* – Witness on the Part of the Community',

International Catholic Review: Communio 15 (1988), 182–98. [HJ 128–9].

10. *Apo.* 44.

11. *Full.* 96.

12. 'Glaubenssinn, Glaubenszustimmung und Glaubenskonsens', *Theologie und Glaube* 69 (1979), 263–71. [HJ 54–5].

13. Rom. 10:17.

14. *Cons.* 73.

15. 'Sensus Fidelium Reconsidered', *New Theology Review* 2 (1989), 48–64. [HJ 130–1].

16. *Concil.* 23–30.

17. '*Sensus Fidelium and Infallibility*', *The American Ecclesiastical Review* 167 (1973), 450–86. [HJ 47–8].

18. J. Feiner and M. Löhrer (eds), *Mysterium Salutis: Grundriss heilsgeschichtlicher Dogmatik* (Einsiedeln: Benziger, 1965), 545–55. [HJ 41–4].

19. *LG* §31.

20. *Christi.* §14, 15.

21. 'Authority, Connatural Knowledge, and the Spontaneous Judgement of the Faithful', *Theological Studies* 29 (1968), 742–51. [HJ 44–5].

22. Glaser's emphasis, but quoting Maritain in *The Range of Reason* (New York: Scribner, 1953), 16. [HJ 58, n. 9].

23. 'Le Peuple de Dieu est-il infaillible? L'Importance du *sensus fidelium* dans l'Église post-conciliaire'. *Freiburger Zeitschrift für Philosophie und Theologie* 35 (1988), 3–19. [HJ 129–30].

24. 'Bedeutung und Begründung des Glaubenssinnes (Sensus fidei) als eines dogmatischen Erkenntniskriteriums', *Catholica* 25 (1971), 271–303. [HJ 45–7].

25. 'Le "*Sensus Fidelium*". Réflexion théologique' in *Foi populaire, foi savante* [Cogitatio fidei, No. 87] (Paris: Cerf, 1976), 9–40. [HJ 48–51].

26. 'Remarques critiques pour une théologie de "consensus fidelium"' in *Foi populaire, foi savante*, 49–60. [HJ 51–2].

27. *Apo.* 239.

28. 'Einleitende Überlegungen zum Verhältnis von Theologie und Volksreligion' in K. Rahner, C. Modehn and M. Göpfert (eds), *Volksreligion – Religion des Volkes* (Stuttgart: Kohlhammer, 1979), 9–16; reprinted in Rahner's *Schriften zur Theologie*, vol. XVI (Zurich: Einsiedeln, 1984), 185–95. [HJ 55–6].

29. 'Offizielle Glaubenslehre der Kirche und faktische Gläubigkeit

des Volkes' in K. Rahner and H. Fries (eds), *Theologie in Freiheit und Verantwortung* (Munich: Kösel, 1984), 15–29. [HJ 56–8].

30. *Concil.*
31. Ibid. ix.
32. Ibid. 3–11.
33. *De praedest. sanct.*, n. 27 (PL xliv, 980).
34. *LG* §35.
35. Ibid.
36. *Concil.* 73–81.
37. Ibid. 82–91.
38. 'Sensus fidelium. Der Theologe zwischen dem Lehramt der Hierarchie und dem Lehramt der Gläubigen' in J. Pfammater and E. Christen (eds), *Theologe und Hierarch* [Theologische Berichte, No. 17] (Zürich: Benziger, 1988), 55–77. [HJ 125–6].
39. *Cons.* 103–4.
40. *LG* §32.

Ch. 3: What Newman Would Say

1. Ian Ker, *Healing the Wound of Humanity* (London: Darton, Longman and Todd Ltd, 1993), 68.
2. Ian Ker, *Newman on Being a Christian* (London: Harper Collins, 1990), 119.
3. Ibid. 48–9.
4. *Full.* 90–1, 92–4.
5. *LG* §8.
6. *PS* iii. 207, 222, 224; v. 41.
7. *Apo.* 224–5.
8. *Full.* 85–6.
9. *Dev.* 38.
10. Quoted from C. S. Dessain, *Newman's Spiritual Themes* (Dublin: Veritas Publications, 1977), 9.
11. *Ari.* 145–6.
12. *GA* 83.
13. *LD* xxiii. 105.
14. *GA* 82.
15. *Ari.* 80–2.
16. *US* 336.
17. Ibid. 316–18.

18. *Dev.* 38. For Newman's concept of an 'idea' see Ian Ker, *John Henry Newman: A Biography* (Oxford, 1990), 302-4.
19. *US* 336.
20. Ibid. 326.
21. *Ess.* ii. 101.
22. *Diff.* ii. 372.
23. *Shape*, 221, quoting E. Hughes, *The Participation of the Faithful in the Regal and Prophetic Mission of Christ According to St Augustine* (Washington, 1956), 50.
24. *LD* xxv. 447.
25. *Diff.* ii. 372.
26. *LD* xxv. 71.
27. *Diff.* ii. 335.
28. Ibid. 320-1.
29. *LD* xxv. 284.
30. *Diff.* ii. 322.
31. *LD* xix. 179-80.
32. *Apo.* 231.
33. *Diff.* ii. 89.
34. *Ess.* ii. 53-4.
35. *VM* 24-7.
36. Ibid. 29, 45.
37. Ibid. 45-6.
38. Ibid. 40-6.
39. *LD* xxv. 31; xxii. 99.
40. *VM* 40-2.
41. *Achiev.* 48.
42. *US* 353-60.
43. *Achiev.* 46-7.
44. *LD* xi. 293; xv. 381.
45. *US* 203-4.
46. *LD* xi. 289.
47. *US* 312-13.
48. *Apo.* 229-30.
49. Ibid. 231.
50. *LD* xix. 179-80.
51. *Apo.* 231.
52. *LD* xix. 179-80.
53. *VM* 29.
54. *Apo.* 235.
55. Ibid. 237-8.

56. Ibid. 225.
57. Ibid. 235–6; 225; 230–1.
58. Ian Ker, *Newman the Theologian: A Reader* (London: Collins, 1990), 47.
59. *Ess.* ii. 53–4.

Ch. 4: History of the *Sensus Fidelium*

1. I owe the insights of this paragraph to Dr Gregory Glazov through personal communication.
2. These and other relevant biblical texts are cited in *Lay People*, 272–3.
3. *Christi.* §14.
4. *Lay People*, 271.
5. Ibid. 273.
6. *Shape*, 221–2, and see n. 23 of ch. 3 above.
7. *Lay People*, 274–5.
8. These and other relevant patristic texts are cited in *Lay People*, 465–7 (Appendix II).
9. *Praescr.*, 28.
10. *Ep. cii* (PG xxxvii, 200).
11. *Adv. Eunomium,* lib. 3, c. 1 (PG xxix. 654).
12. *Adv. Haer. Panar.,* haer. 78, c. 6 (PG xlii, 705).
13. Quoted by R. Wherlé in *De la coutume en droit canonique*, Paris, 1928, p. 75, n. 1.
14. *Contra Crescon.*, lib. 2, c. 32 (PL xliii, 490); *De bapt. contra Donat.*, lib. 2, c. 9, n. 14 (PL xliii, 135).
15. *De dono persev.*, c. 23, n. 63 (PL xlv, 1031); *De natura et gratia,* n. 52 (PL xliv, 272).
16. *De praedest. sanct.*, n. 27 (PL xliv, 980).
17. *Sermo ccxciv*, c. 17 (PL xxxviii, 1346); *De peccat. meritis et remiss.*, lib. 1, c. 24, n. 34 (PL xliv, 128).
18. In Session xiii, c. 1 (Denzinger, 874).
19. *The Documents of Vatican II*, Walter M. Abbott, gen. ed. (London-Dublin: Geoffrey Chapman, 1966), 1–7.
20. *LG* §10–13.
21. Ibid. §12.

Ch. 5: The Laity

1. *LD* xix, 414.
2. I obtained this biographical information from Fr Aidan Nichols' work, *From Newman to Congar: The Idea of Doctrinal Development from the Victorians to the Second Vatican Council* (Edinburgh: T&T Clark, 1991), which see for further details.
3. Congar's works include: *Chrétiens en dialogue. Contributions catholiques à l'Oecuménisme* (1964), ix-lxiv; *La Foi et la téologie* (1968); *La Tradition et la vie de l'Eglise* (1984).
4. Aidan Nichols' works include: *The Thought of Pope Benedict XVI: An Introduction to the Theology of Joseph Ratzinger* (2007); *The Shape of Catholic Theology: An Introduction to its Sources, Principles and History* (1991); *Christendom Awake: On Re-Energising the Church in Culture* (1999).
5. *Lay People*, 3.
6. *LG* §31.
7. See especially *Christi*. §14.
8. *LG* §30-1.
9. *Christi*. §14-15.
10. Ibid. 14, citing *LG* §12, 35.
11. *Lay People*, Appendix II, n. 1.
12. Ibid. 288.
13. *Shape*, 221-3.
14. *LG* §25.
15. *Lay People*, 290.
16. Ibid. 289. In quotations from Congar in this chapter, the italics are his.

Ch. 6: *On Consulting the Faithful in Matters of Doctrine*

1. Republished in the 1961 Coulson edition (*Cons.*).
2. For a fuller account see Coulson's Introduction at *Cons*. 9-13.
3. *LD* xix. 10-11.
4. Ibid. xviii. 547.
5. Ibid. xix. 129-30.
6. Ibid. 135.
7. Ibid. 140-1.
8. Ibid. 149-50.
9. Ibid. xxix. 426.

10. *Cons.* 36.
11. Ibid. 54–5.
12. Ibid. 60–2.
13. Ibid. 62–3.
14. Ibid. 63–4.
15. Ibid. 65–70.
16. Ibid. 70–2.
17. Arianism: A heresy of the fourth century, named after Arius, a priest of Alexandria. He argued that, as there can be only one God, the Father alone possesses the divine nature: thus, his Son, Christ, must have been 'created' and therefore be subordinate to him and less than a God, a kind of demigod.
18. *Cons.* 73–5.
19. Ibid. 74–5.
20. *Cons.* 75–7.
21. Ibid. 102–3.
22. Ibid. 77–9.
23. Ibid. 84.
24. Ibid. 85.
25. Ibid. 86–7.
26. Ibid. 90–1.
27. Ibid. 94–5.
28. Ibid. 88–9.
29. Ibid. 103–5.
30. Ibid. 105–6.
31. Ibid. 77.
32. *LD* xix. 206–7.
33. Reprinted in *Cons.* 109–18.
34. *Cons.* 115–18.
35. Ibid. 112–13.
36. *Lay People*, 285–6.
37. *Cons.* 109–10.
38. Newman is a lawyer manqué in a real sense. He was admitted to Lincoln's Inn on 19 November 1819 but had his name taken off its books on 20 April 1825. The Inn have no record of his ever having kept term there. However, after the Second World War when the heraldic glass in the Great Hall was replaced, his arms were placed in the window dedicated to past members of the Inn distinguished in fields other than the law.

Ch. 7: The *Sensus Fidelium* and Opposition to the Magisterium

1. *On the Regulation of Birth: (Humanae Vitae)* Encyclical Letter of Pope Paul VI (1968) §11, 12, 14.
2. *CCC* 1956.
3. *Famil.* §4.
4. Pope John Paul II in address of 17 September 1983.
5. *Famil.* §5.
6. *Shape*, 229–30 (referring to *Cons.* 72).
7. Pius XI, Encyc. *Casti Connubii*, 31 September 1930.
8. *TTB* 378–80.
9. Ibid. 390.
10. Ibid. 333–6
11. Ibid. 378.
12. John Paul speaks of the body as the 'expression of the person'. Thus, the 'language of the body' is not confined to the conjugal relationship; celibacy for the sake of the kingdom is equally 'language of the body'.
13. *TTB* 354–7.
14. The word *sarx* (flesh) as used by St Paul is not to be identified exclusively with the physical body. Its meaning is the self, including physical and psychical elements as vehicles of the outward life and lower levels of experience. 'It is man in his humanness with all the limitations, moral weakness, vulnerability, creatureliness and morality, which being human implies ...' Quoted in footnotes to *TTB* 229–30 (where a fuller account of the interpretation of *sarx* is given) from R. E. O. White, *Biblical Ethics* [Exeter: Paternoster Press, 1979], 135–8.
15. *TTB* 355.
16. John Paul uses the expression 'the author of the Ephesians' alternately with 'the Apostle' and 'St Paul' having in mind that the Pauline authorship of Ephesians is disputed among exegetes. (*TTB* 380, 1st footnote).
17. *TTB* 378.
18. Ibid. 378–9.
19. Ibid. 379.
20. For studies of the natural law and objective morality see essays by John Finnis and William E. May in *Principles of Catholic Moral Life*, ed. William E. May (Chicago: Franciscan Herald Press, 1981), 113–190. Also Lawler, 58–65.

21. Pope Paul VI, Address to the Teams of Our Lady, Rome, 4 May 1970.
22. *TTB* 16. This summary is supplied by John S. Grabowski in a Foreword to *TTB*.
23. See Paul M. Quay's analysis in *Why Humanae Vitae was Right*, ed. Janet E. Smith (San Francisco: Ignatius Press, 1993), 19–45.

Ch. 8: A Last Reflection with Newman

1. *Famil.* §6.
2. Newman was beatified on 19 September 2010.
3. Raniero Cantalamessa, *Life in the Lordship of Christ: A Spiritual Commentary on the Letter to the Romans*, (London: Darton, Longman and Todd, 1989), 240.
4. *GA* 72, 74–6.
5. Lawler, 66.
6. *GA* 252–3, 256.
7. *Apo.* 217.
8. *PS* v. 314–16.
9. Lawler, 156–7.
10. *Shape*, 229–30.
11. Karl Rahner, 'The Encyclical *Humanae Vitae*', *Theological Investigations* (New York: Seabury, 1974), vol. II, 284–5. Cited by Ralph M. McInerny in *What Went Wrong with Vatican II*, (Manchester, New Hampshire: Sophia Institute Press, 1998), 149.
12. *LD* xx. 430.
13. Aidan Nichols, *Christendom Awake*, (Edinburgh: T&T Clark, 1999), 48.
14. Ian Ker, *John Henry Newman: A Biography*, (Oxford: Clarendon Press, 1988), 60.
15. *The Idea of a University*, ed. I. T. Ker (Oxford: Clarendon Press, 1976), 285.
16. *Apo.* 225.
17. Ibid. 116. This quotation is from Newman's description of his first, fleeting apprehension, while still an Anglican, that the Church of Rome is the Church of antiquity, the one true Church, because 'the deliberate judgement, in which the whole Church at length rests and acquiesces, is an infallible prescription and a final sentence against such portions of it as protest and secede'.